The Culture of Death

The Culture of Death

BENJAMIN NOYS

Oxford • New York

First published in 2005 by

Berg

Editorial offices:

1st Floor, Angel Court, 81 St Clements Street, Oxford OX4 1AW, UK

175 Fifth Avenue, New York, NY 10010, USA

Berg is the imprint of Oxford International Publishers Ltd.

Library of Congress Cataloging-in-Publication Data

Noys, Benjamin, 1969-

    The culture of death / Benjamin Noys.

      p. cm.

    Includes bibliographical references and index.

  I. Death--Social aspects. 2. Civilization, Modern--21st century. I. Title.

HQ1073.N69 2005

306.9'09182'1--dc22

                      2004026842

British Library Cataloguing-in-Publication Data

A catalogue record for this book is available from the British Library.

ISBN-13 978 184520 068 8 (Cloth)

  ISBN-10 1 84520 068 3 (Cloth)

    ISBN-13 978 184520 069 5 (Paper)

    ISBN-10 1 84520 069 1 (Paper)

Typeset by JS Typesetting Ltd, Porthcawl, Mid Glamorgan.

Printed in the United Kingdom by Biddles Ltd, King's Lynn.

www.bergpublishers.com

Contents

Abbreviations

References to works by Giorgio Agamben:

Homo Sacer: Sovereign Power and Bare Life (HS)

Means without End: Notes on Politics (ME)

Potentialities: Collected Essays in Philosophy (P)

Remnants of Auschwitz: the Witness and the Archive (RA)

Acknowledgements

Tristan Palmer's editorial assistance and enthusiasm have been essential to this project, as has the work of all those at Berg. I am grateful to University College Chichester for providing teaching relief to allow the completion of this book. I would like to thank those who took time to read all or part of the manuscript: Jane Gillett, James Tink, Hugo Frey and Fiona Price. I would also like to thank the publisher's reviewer for their comments on the book. My family and friends have given me invaluable support during the writing of this work.

Introduction: Exposed to Death

How can we understand the culture of death today? P. D. James (b. 1920) is one of the most widely respected of contemporary British crime writers. In her novel *The Black Tower* the detective hero Adam Dalgliesh considers just this question: 'Now that death had replaced sex as the great unmentionable it had acquired its own prudency; to die when you had not yet become a nuisance and before your friends could reasonably raise the ritual chant of "happy release" was in the worst of taste' (1977: 9). He expresses the common perception that death is replacing sex as the new taboo subject in modern culture. However, if death is taboo and we are less comfortable at dealing with death than previous generations, then why is crime fiction, which is relentlessly focused on death, so popular? P. D. James, for example, is well known for her graphic descriptions of dead bodies and for creating hideously baroque murders. Also, if death is so taboo then how do we account for the fact that the media continues to give us increasingly explicit representations of death? The television images and photographs of the victims of the attack on the World Trade Center throwing themselves to certain death to avoid being burned alive are only one recent and traumatic example of our exposure to death in contemporary culture.

The idea that modern death is taboo is one that has become entrenched in popular understanding, despite many criticisms. What is the usual story? To take the example of Britain, during the nineteenth century the Victorian way of death put an emphasis on the family farewell for the dying and a complex culture of mourning with ostentatious displays of grief (see Jalland, 1999). Far from death being taboo there was even a widespread children's literature designed to help prepare them for the possibility of their own early death. Also photographs of the dead would be taken as a form of remembrance, which often seem macabre to contemporary taste, especially when they show babies and children.[1] This Victorian celebration of death would disappear under the impact of the decline in Christian belief and the decline of the death rate. What was also important was the effect of the First World War, when the mass death of young men 'shattered what remained of the Victorian way of death for many families' (Jalland, 1999: 251). The vast numbers of deaths, and the problems of recovering and identifying the remains of the dead, destroyed the possibility of mourning.

Another factor, which has not been widely discussed, is the possible effect of the influenza epidemic after the First World War, which killed more people than the war itself. This 'forgotten epidemic' may also have altered attitudes to the commemoration and mourning for the dead. In the twentieth century the Victorian way of death was often dismissed for exemplifying the worst of Victorian faults: 'hypocrisy, formality, social conformism, tasteless ostentation, and morbid emotionalism' (Houlbrooke, 1998: 375). Oscar Wilde represented this new attitude when he commented on the sentimental death scene of Little Nell in Charles Dickens's novel *The Old Curiosity Shop* (1840–41): 'one must have a heart of stone to read the death of Little Nell without laughing'. In contrast to the Victorians' celebration of death, modern death has become isolated within hospitals or residential homes for the elderly, and mourning rituals have largely disappeared or are seen as pathological. The result is what the French historian of death Philippe Ariès has called 'the invisible death' or the 'forbidden death' (1974, 1981). Where once death was accepted as a necessary event, now it is regarded as terrifying. However, the cliché of death as taboo does not really account for all the features of our modern culture of death.

Recently it has been argued that we are witnessing the end of the death taboo (Berridge, 2002). Our 'prudery' in regard to death has been replaced by a new fearless exploration of death in modern culture. As, in the 1960s, sexual liberation challenged the taboos around sex so, in the 1990s and in the new millennium, a new movement of 'death liberation' has arisen that challenges the taboos around death. The effects of AIDS, the 'death awareness' movement, and new explicit representations of death in art and the media have all helped to bring an end to the shame that had become attached to death. Therefore our fascination with representations of death and our exposure to such representations by the media would be another sign of the end of the death taboo. Yet, as the literary critic Jonathan Dollimore has pointed out in his book *Death, Desire and Loss in Western Culture*, this argument is simplistic (1998: 126). The idea that death is taboo in modern culture or the idea that we are now witnessing the end of the death taboo fail both to deal with the complex ways in which death is invisible and highly visible in modern culture.

While in the affluent cultures of the West death has become less visible, due to the decline in death rates and our new prudery around death, we are still exposed to death every day through the media. Despite the fact that there has not yet been a world war since 1945 we all live under the abstract threat of nuclear destruction, which threatens the survival of humanity. Also, advances in science may have reduced the risk of early death in the West but we still experience acute anxieties about ecological catastrophe, the emergence of new and untreatable epidemic diseases and the effects of pollution and waste on our environment. In modern culture death is not simply invisible or taboo but bound up with new structures that expose us to death. It is precisely the issue of our exposure to death that this book explores as the key to analysing the culture of death. Of course, human beings have been, and always are, exposed to death, but does this exposure to death take new forms in modern culture? To analyse death in terms of exposure is also to move beyond the clichés of death as taboo or the end of the death taboo and into the contradictory and uncertain space of death in modern culture.

Why would our sense of being exposed to death have changed? The French theorist and critic of technology Paul Virilio (b. 1932) has called the twentieth century the century of the '*mass production of corpses*' (2002: 14). While it may be true that death has become invisible in certain ways in contemporary Western culture we also have to account for the reality and visibility of the threat of death on an industrial scale. After the Holocaust and during a century of genocides and mass exterminations, from Cambodia to Rwanda, it is difficult to claim that death is now 'invisible' or 'forbidden'. Instead our exposure to death takes the form of being exposed to the possibility of death organised politically, through bureaucratic planning and governmental intervention (Bauman, 1991). Not only that but there are the more banal ways in which we are exposed to death, such as through the car crash; in 2000 more than 116,000 people died in car crashes last year in the 26 OECD countries for which figures are available, an average of 320 deaths a day.

A useful example to introduce the strangely contradictory nature of death in modern culture is the scandal caused by the public autopsy performed on British television by Professor Gunther von Hagens on 20 November 2002 (Miah, 2003). This was the first public autopsy performed in Britain for nearly 200 years and it was widely criticised for trivialising death and abusing the dignity owed to the dead. Von Hagens was already a highly controversial figure for his 'Body Worlds' exhibition, in which real human bodies are displayed that have been preserved through a process that leaves the bodies with the clear appearance of being real. Although Hagens claims an educational purpose for his exhibition and for the autopsy, critics have suggested it is more of a performance or an artistic act. Here we can see the issues concerning the invisibility of death, our discomfort with the dead body, but also our fascination for the display of death, a very visible dead body taken apart before our very eyes on the television screen. In fact, the Greek word 'autopsy' means seeing with one's own eyes.[2]

This strange simultaneous invisibility and visibility of death in modern culture has often been explored by contemporary art, literature and film. Therefore, I shall often turn to works from both high and popular culture to analyse modern death. This book will also use a range of theorists and writers whose work deals with modern death but which have not been widely discussed. The central aim is to grasp what, if anything, is distinctive about our culture of death? I begin, in Chapter One, with an analysis of the time of death. This involves two problems: first, what is our individual experience of exposure to death in modern culture and then, secondly, how can this individual experience be linked to wider social and cultural changes in our exposure to death? These problems will require a new approach to the modern culture of death that can link together these two issues. Then, in Chapter Two, the exposure to death will be analysed in terms of space rather than time. I shall argue that the spaces in which we are exposed to death are also spaces of power, and that we must understand the nature of modern power to understand the nature of modern death. This will involve close analysis of the Nazi concentration and extermination camps as spaces of power that are also spaces of death.

One space of our exposure to death, which seems to characterise modern death in particular, is the hospital room. In Chapter Three I shall examine the debates on life-support and transplant technology to raise again the problems of how we decide on the time of death and who decides on the time of death that I have previously addressed. Instead of seeing modern death being the result of the medicalisation of death I will propose that medicine takes over the power to decide on life and death that had been the domain of the head of state. Doctors are in competition with other figures, such as lawyers, priests, philosophers and the relatives of the ill, for the power to decide on life and death. What is attempted in the first three chapters of the book is a preliminary characterisation of some of the features of the modern culture of death. Alongside this, though, we must also be cautious in claiming any total or complete rupture with previous cultures of death. In fact, many of the features of the culture of modern death suggest a strong continuity with the past. However, the particular nature of our exposure to death in modern culture helps to make clearer the political dimension of death.

The second half of the book is an exploration of possible responses to these new forms of exposure to modern death. Chapter Four examines the attempt to construct an ethical response to the rise of medical power in deciding on life and death. The new philosophical discipline of bioethics sets out to deal with these issues and create an ethical framework for advising medical professionals. Recent critiques of the turn to ethics and the downgrading of the political in contemporary philosophy suggest that we should approach bioethics with caution. In reducing death to an ethical question, issues of politics and power are not given adequate weight. A similar problem is identified in Chapter Five, which looks at the fascination with death in modern art. Again, although modern art seems to be fearlessly exploring death, it has often exploited the shock value of representations of death. This representation of death as transgressive or rule breaking fails to consider how death is a question of power. In Chapter Six then, I turn to the attempts to construct a political resistance to modern death and modern power. Here the figure of the refugee is crucial. The refugee is the person who lacks a national identity and a state to protect his or her political rights. As such the refugee is particularly vulnerable and it is this vulnerability that offers us resources for trying to find a new politics that might challenge our exposure to death.

Finally, in the conclusion, I address the question of the different meanings that have been attached to death. The constant search for the meaning of death in Western culture may well be misplaced. Instead of focusing on the meaning of death a new approach is taken which examines death in terms of the experience of our exposure to death. If we are exposed to death then we cannot avoid the question of death itself or take shelter in the desire to give a meaning to death. Instead, death appears as something that resists being treated as either meaningful or meaningless. In thinking through the culture of death in terms of our being exposed to death, new paths open for critical analysis and thinking. Although this work is focused on 'modern death' the questions that it raises also force us to consider more generally how we might go about approaching death. In particular it is important to resist simply becoming fascinated by death. Our ongoing fascination with death is something to be analysed rather than celebrated, and this work is a contribution to that critical analysis.

The central concern that has motivated my writing of this book has been to analyse our exposure to death in modern culture, and the link between this exposure to death and our exposure to power. Recent events have only given more weight to this concern: the American war on Afghanistan and the American invasion and occupation of Iraq have both been justified in terms of a new global 'war on terrorism'. The promise is of further interventions against the 'axis of evil' or any other state, group or individual that threatens American or Western security. These new forms of warfare and these new extensions of state power on a global scale leave anyone who is identified as a 'terrorist' exposed to death. Often these military interventions have been accompanied by humanitarian aid. Whatever the intentions of this aid it creates a new series of people exposed to death and reduced to the categories of refugees, starving victims or injured children. The American critic Noam Chomsky has described this as the 'new military humanism' (1999), in which military power is combined with 'humanitarian' aid to justify Western interventions. Although this aid may set out to relieve the plight of those left exposed to death, it can actually work alongside power and support it. This book has been written in the time of this emergence of global power and it is, I consider, a sign of hope that this power has been confronted with mass global protest on the streets of the world's cities. Although critical analysis is essential, it is in these spaces that global power will truly be contested.

NOTES

1. American examples of these photographs of the dead can be found in Michael Lesy's 1973 book *Wisconsin Death Trip* (2000), since made into a film of the same name directed by James Marsh (1999).
2. The American avant-garde film-maker Stan Brakhage's *The Act of Seeing with One's Own Eyes* (1971) is a film of three autopsies, taking its title from the original Greek meaning of the word.

CHAPTER I

A New Time of Death?

INTRODUCTION: APPROACHING DEATH

Have we entered a new time of death? Is there a particular form of modern death and does this new form of modern death mean that we experience our own time of death in a different way? To answer these questions we need to grasp the nature of death. In general the academic approach to death has been focused on studying 'the ways death has been represented' (Goodwin and Bronfen, 1993: 4). Instead of analysing what death actually is, or might be, it examines the cultural and historical meanings of death. Although it accepts that death is biological or physical, the concern is more with analysing the meanings attached to death and with seeing death as a cultural and historical product. If we were to take this approach to the question of modern death, then we would ask what meanings are attached to death today, and how those meanings differ from those attached to death previously. Such an approach is common in what has often been called 'death studies', which is the attempt to draw together a whole range of work done on death across a range of academic disciplines, from history to philosophy, cultural studies to literary criticism, into a new interdisciplinary academic field.

Whether death studies yet constitutes a fully-fledged discipline is highly debatable; at the moment it seems more of a proposal than a reality. The claim that underpins this model is that death has no inner essence or fixed meaning and that we can only study its outward manifestations: the meaning or meanings attached to death. Jonathan Dollimore has criticised death studies for its failure to ask the question of death itself (1998: 127). In this way it is very similar to cultural studies in general, which tends to favour analysing the historical conditions out of which concepts emerge rather than trying to discuss the truth of these concepts. Instead of asking 'What is death?' the question that is asked is 'How is death represented in particular discourses?' In addition, although the question of death itself is left unanswered, these approaches have a surprising confidence in their ability to determine the meanings attached to death. In fact the question of death is far harder to grasp than they suppose. If all cultures organise mourning rituals, sacrifices and the forms of relationship between the living and the dead, then any culture can be considered as a culture of death (Derrida, 1993: 43).

If we are to describe the cultural or historical meanings that have been attached to death, it is very difficult to draw a limit around what we might discuss. The cultural meaning of death touches on nearly every aspect of a culture, running through it in various ways, and when we try to analyse death we find ourselves faced with a 'huge archive' (Derrida, 1993: 80). One way in which to narrow down this huge archive is to examine the particular way a culture organises this relationship to death and the dead. Although each culture deals with death, each culture deals with death in a different way (Derrida, 1993: 43). If we are trying to analyse modern death then we should analyse how modern culture organises our relation to death and the division between life and death. This allows us to understand if there is anything distinctive about the modern culture of death, either in relation to the past or in relation to other cultures. To do this I shall take up the question of the time of death, the moment when our culture defines the transition from life to death. This requires that we not only analyse what death might be but also explore the concept of life. The definition of death, I shall argue, depends on the definition of life.

To define death we must analyse the strange border between life and death. In the American writer Edgar Allan Poe's (1809–1849) short story 'The Premature Burial' (1844) the narrator says 'The boundaries which divide Life from Death, are at best shadowy and vague' (1993: 290). How are we to understand the time of death in modern culture if this boundary is so shadowy? The approach of this book is one that examines more closely the question of death itself and the processes by which the boundary is drawn between life and death, in particular in modern culture. To do this I shall use the work of the contemporary Italian philosopher Giorgio Agamben.

Originally his work was preoccupied with issues around aesthetics, literature and philosophy but then in his book *Homo Sacer: Sovereign Power and Bare Life* (1998) he took up the question of life in Western culture. What he finds at the centre of Western culture is a form of life called 'bare life' (*vita nuda*), which is a form of life that is exposed to death.[1] This is life that is left exposed to death by power, and so the shadowy border between life and death is a political matter. The decision on the time of death, on when we are living and when we must die, is, Agamben will argue, fundamentally political.

As well as focusing on the modern culture of death this study will also be focusing on this in culture in the West, and, in particular, Britain and the United States. This is another limit, omitting as it does the experience of other cultures. There is also the risk of suggesting that Western culture itself is a homogeneous whole, rather than being hybrid and in constant interchange with other cultures. Postcolonial critics have rightly insisted that the dominance of Western culture needs to be put into question. What I hope this study will demonstrate is that the analysis of the Western way of death is vital because it is in the process of imposing itself over the world, and that this is the result of political power and not of any supposed 'natural superiority' of Western culture. Also, this study will interrogate the limits of the Western culture of death, and challenge these limits.

Agamben suggests, as we shall see, that the history of Western culture can be understood as the history of bare life. Bare life, life exposed to death, is the crucial political concept for the West. Although bare life has always been at the centre of Western culture, today the exposure to death is taking on new and more extreme forms. Agamben argues that Western culture has become thanatopolitical, which means that it is dominated by a politics of death that leaves us more and more exposed to both death and the operations of power. This is a controversial and provocative claim that has been widely discussed and criticised, but it is yet to have had a great deal of impact within the field of death studies. In this chapter, Agamben's history of the West as a history of bare life is set out and then some of the criticisms that he has provoked explored. The importance of his work is that it allows us to question some of the assumptions of death studies but we must also critically question his understanding of modern death.

First, however, I turn to one attempt to grasp modern culture as a culture in which we are exposed to death in new ways. Although, as Edgar Allan Poe's short story pointed out in 1845, the border between life and death has always been shadowy and vague, Agamben sees this situation as getting worse in modern culture. This is because today our culture and our politics have put the time of death into question. To grasp why Agamben might make this argument we need to look at the new experiences of being exposed to death in modern culture. In particular, it is the fact that we live in the wake of the concentration camps and under the threat of nuclear war that seems to expose us to the threat of mass death. As the historian R. J. B. Bosworth (1994) has said, we must examine how we can explain Auschwitz and Hiroshima, the two key 'symbols' of this threat. What psychological and cultural effects does this threat of mass anonymous extinction have? Do these threats mean that we now live within a new modern culture of death? To answer these questions we can examine one manifesto of the culture of modern death.

A MANIFESTO OF MODERN DEATH

In 1957 the American novelist Norman Mailer (b. 1923) published his essay 'The White Negro'. Already acclaimed for his novel *The Naked and the Dead* (1948), based on his experience of combat in the Second World War, he now took up the role of social critic. Along with the 'Beat writers', Mailer called for a rebellion against the stifling conformity of postwar American culture. In Mailer's case he found his rebel hero in the psychopath, that type of criminal who lives without guilt and who acts on his desires without caring for the consequences. The 'white Negro' would combine the guilt-free nature of the psychopath with a rebellion against social control. He would also take as his model the 'cool' attitude of African-American street culture, which had its own language and norms outside conventional mainstream America. What is particularly fascinating is that this new sense of rebellion is the result of changing attitudes to death. Although 'The White Negro' is a manifesto of cultural rebellion, which predicts the youth movements of the 1960s, it can also be considered as a manifesto of modern death. The question that Mailer focuses on is the question of the time of death and whether we have, any longer, a secure or stable time of death.

This problem of the time of death is expressed clearly in the lengthy opening paragraph of his essay, which is worth quoting in full:

> Probably, we will never be able to determine the psychic havoc of the concentration camps and the atom bomb upon the unconscious mind of almost everyone alive in these years. For the first time in civilized history, perhaps for the first time in all of history, we have been forced to live with the suppressed knowledge that the smallest facets of our personality or the most minor projection of our ideas, or indeed the absence of ideas and the absence of personality could mean equally well that we might still be doomed to die as a cipher in some vast statistical operation in which our teeth would be counted, and our hair would be saved, but our death itself would be unknown, unhonoured, and unremarked, a death which could not follow with dignity as a possible consequence to serious actions we had chosen, but rather a death by *deus ex machina* in a gas chamber or radioactive city; and so if in the midst of civilization – that civilization founded upon the Faustian urge to dominate nature by mastering time, mastering the links of social cause and effect – in the middle of an economic civilization founded upon the confidence that time could be subjected to our will, our psyche was subjected itself to the intolerable anxiety that death being causeless, life was causeless as well, and time deprived of cause and effect had come to a stop. (Mailer 1968: 270)

In this opening paragraph Mailer is trying to assess the psychic effects of the concentration camps and the threat of nuclear war on modern culture. He suggests that the major effect of these events is to dislocate our sense of having a proper time of death. As the sense of the time of death is dislocated then so is our sense of time more generally: if we cannot master the time of death then we cannot master time and our culture is thrown into crisis.

The reason for this is that death is no longer necessarily an individual matter, but now it can be the result of a vast and anonymous operation carried out upon us. In the face of this collective mass death, whatever we have done or might do in life is of no significance, and we are exposed to a death that is 'unknown, unhonoured, and unremarked'. Although our death might be counted or recorded in such an operation it is a death that does not count for anything. As the Soviet dictator Josef Stalin (1879–1953), who presided over the mass death inflicted during collectivisation and the purges, once said: 'A single death is a tragedy, a million deaths is a statistic.' This exposure to mass death alters our experience of the time of death because death can no longer be the result of our actions, and so we have lost control over death, if, of course, we ever had such control. In the Middle Ages the ambition was to achieve a 'good death', and practical instruction manuals in the techniques of dying well, the *ars moriendi*, were written to this end. What inspired horror was a sudden and unprepared death (*mors improvisa*), but today, according to Mailer, that is becoming the dominant form of modern death.

This new form of death produces an 'intolerable anxiety', as we have to live with the knowledge that we are always exposed to mass anonymous death. This is not simply the anonymous death of the epidemic or war, but a deliberate and organised death, a kind of 'rational' or industrialised death at the hands of bureaucratic planners. As the historian of the Holocaust Raul Hilberg has noted, 'Never before in history had people been killed on an assembly-line basis' (1985: 221). In the light of this possible fate, and the possibility of extinction due to nuclear war, Mailer proposes that today we live life that is already saturated with the threat of death. We live under a death sentence that has already been passed. Like the character Joseph K. in Franz Kafka's (1883–1924) novel *The Trial* (1925), we can, at any moment, be taken out to die like a dog. Is it true, however, that we are more exposed to death today than in the past? At least in the affluent West declining mortality rates would suggest that we are less at risk from death than in the past. What Mailer is referring to, though, are the new forms of exposure to death that have come to threaten us. These new forms of mass death rely on techniques of planning, statistical calculation and population control that have been developed in modernity. In particular, the threat of nuclear war exposes us all, potentially, to death. It seems that in modern culture our political systems constantly put our lives in question.

Also, and this is a problem to which I shall return, although there may be new forms of exposure to death, this exposure to death is not evenly distributed. For those who live in the 'third world', a phrase still used to describe those non-industrialised, ex-colonial or developing countries outside the West, the exposure to death is far more extensive. Mortality due to illness, from cholera to AIDS, starvation and political violence is an ever-present threat for much of the world's population. However, even in the affluent West we are still exposed to death in new ways and, as the war in the former Yugoslavia made clear, concentration camps and mass executions can return in Europe. What is particularly useful about Mailer's work, although it expresses the situation in an extreme way, is that it grasps how the threat of exposure to mass death can alter the individual's experience of death. The border between life and death is not only a collective matter for our culture but it is also experienced at the level of the individual.

When we talk about the time of death we are talking about the time of the death in two senses. We are talking about the time of death in the sense of an age or epoch or culture of death. This is the periodisation of death, such as the idea that we now live in a new modern culture of death that has eclipsed the previous Victorian culture of death. The second sense is of our individual time of when we shall actually die. I am following Mailer in linking these two senses together and of playing with the ambiguity of the phrase 'time of death'. What Mailer points out is that the new time of death, in the sense of a new modern period of death lived under the threat of nuclear war and the concentration camps, alters our own time of death, in terms of our individual experience. When discussing the 'time of death' both these senses must be borne in mind, as well as the new links that have been made between them in modern culture.

Mailer suggests that we have entered a new time of death, of modern death, and the symptom of this is that our individual death has become meaningless. There are, however, some problems with his attempt to grasp modern death, beyond those I have already mentioned. The major one is that, although he alerts us to the individual's experience of death, Mailer does not move beyond an explanation in individual terms. For him it is taken as given that the concentration camps and the threat of nuclear war have altered the nature of death and we are only left with the problem of how we might respond to this new situation. There is no real attempt to properly grasp whether modern death is really a new time of death and how that might have come about. Also, he presumes that once we find ourselves in this situation we are forced to accept it. Mailer writes that if we 'live with death from adolescence to premature senescence, why then the only life-giving answer is to accept the terms of death' (1968: 271).

All we are left with is the opportunity to become the 'white Negro', someone who is capable of accepting the threat of death and living with it. In fact, Mailer even celebrates this new situation of modern death, writing that 'No matter what its horrors the twentieth century is a vastly exciting century for its tendency to reduce all of life to its ultimate alternatives' (1968: 288). He seems to be excited by the possibilities of living in a culture of modern death but he offers us no real explanation of how we have arrived at this point. This is why we must now look at Giorgio Agamben's attempt to write the history of the West as the history of life left exposed to death. He offers us a more precise way of grasping just how we are exposed to death today. However, his work is controversial and I want to locate it in relation to another provocative analysis of modern death offered by the contemporary French theorist Jean Baudrillard (b. 1929). This comparison will then lead us into consideration of some of the criticisms that have been offered of Agamben's history of bare life. He does not provide us with the definitive account of the culture of death in the West, but his arguments challenge us to think about modern death in new ways.

A SHORT HISTORY OF BARE LIFE

Agamben tries to provide us with a history of life and death through the concept of bare life, of life exposed to death. His work is driven by the desire to engage with the current situation of bare life today. He argues that Western culture has been brought to the edge of catastrophe by its exposure of life to death. However, we cannot respond to this situation by appealing to some sort of individual solution, like the 'white Negro', which would allow us to live with this crisis. Instead we must explore the politics of life and death in modern culture, which has been left largely unexamined. He begins at a somewhat surprising point: with an obscure figure from Ancient Roman law called the *homo sacer* or sacred man. The sacred man is a figure who is left exposed to death, but he is exposed in a particular way. Roman law defines him as someone who may be killed and yet not sacrificed. To be defined as the sacred man is an act of punishment, but it is a punishment of a strange type. Anyone can kill the sacred man without being punished for it, so the sacred man has been placed outside the protection of law. At the same time, however, he cannot be sacrificed in a religious ceremony, so the sacred man is excluded from the religious domain as well. Agamben will argue that this figure, left exposed to death outside human and religious law, is not just a figure that belongs to the past. Instead, according to Agamben, the sacred man still performs an essential function in modern politics as well (HS: 8). He is the first figure of bare life, of life left exposed to death.

The decision to define someone as the sacred man is political; it is an act of power that places him outside the law. We are used to thinking of the idea of life as sacred as meaning that life is to be preserved at all costs. When those who belong to the anti-abortion movement talk of the sacredness of life or of the rights of the unborn child, they are arguing against any termination of pregnancy as the ending of life. However, what Agamben suggests is that when life is defined as sacred under Ancient Roman law it is actually life that is left totally exposed to death. Sacred life is not life that is protected from death but life that is vulnerable to death and which lacks any social or cultural protection against death. This withdrawal of legal and religious protection is, Agamben argues, an act of power. In particular it is an act of sovereign power, that power which is usually seen as belonging to the head of state (the sovereign). It is this act of exposing life to death, of defining life as bare life, which makes the decision on the border between life and death political. What sovereign power does is to produce life as bare life.

So 'from the beginning this sacred life has an eminently political character' (HS: 100) because it is defined as such by a political decision. This means that bare life, life exposed to death, and sovereign power, that which exposes life to death, are always linked together. In this chapter I am going to follow Agamben's history of bare life and then in Chapter Two I shall deal in more detail with sovereign power as a kind of space of power. The importance of this history of bare life is that it concerns the decision on the time of death and it will help us to grasp whether that decision has changed in modern culture. Although it might seem that the sacred man is simply left outside the political and cultural order Agamben will argue that

this abandonment of the sacred man is still a political act. The exposing of
the sacred man to the threat of death by withdrawing legal and religious
protection leaves him completely exposed to power. This is not so much the
exclusion of the sacred man from society but his inclusion within the space
of power. As Agamben writes, 'human life is included in the political order
in being exposed to an unconditional capacity to be killed' (HS: 85).

How are we to understand this strange situation by which the sacred man
is excluded from society but then somehow included within the space of
power? Agamben calls this process 'inclusive exclusion': the process by which
life is included within the political order as its hidden foundation but only
by the act of seeming to exclude it from legal and religious protection. It is
this process which Agamben sees as central to Western culture and which
constitutes the definition of death as a political matter. To argue this he
has to establish why the obscure figure of the sacred man might have any
relevance today. We might well be sceptical, and critics certainly have been,
of why this figure should be the means of making 'the very codes of political
power ... unveil their mysteries' (HS: 8), as Agamben claims. Certainly the
sacred man exists as a figure of Roman law but does this figure continue to
play a role in later legal and social systems? In particular, can we establish
the place of the figure of the sacred man in modern culture?

To answer these questions we must follow Agamben's rather brief history
of Western culture as the history of the reappearance of the sacred man and
bare life. From the sacred man of Roman law Agamben then jumps to the
figure of the bandit in the Middle Ages. The importance of the bandit is
that, like the sacred man, he is left exposed to death by an act of sovereign
power. The word 'bandit' originally derives from the Italian *bandito*, meaning
'banned'. So the bandit is someone who has been banned, that is excluded,
from the political order. In this act of banning, which is carried out by the
sovereign, the head of state, the bandit is left exposed to the threat of being
killed. The bandit has forfeited all his rights and is left in the same state as
that of the sacred man: reduced to bare life. In fact in older Germanic and
Anglo-Saxon sources the bandit is often defined as the 'wolf-man' (*wargus*,
werwolf) from which the French *loup garou* or 'werewolf' is derived (HS: 105).
The bandit has not only lost his political rights and social identity but
has also become defined as subhuman. This habit of defining criminals as

sub-human actually still persists today in the American choice to define those criminals known as the worst of the worst as 'super-predators', that is, as vicious animals. The exclusion of the criminal from the community seems to cost them their humanity and leave them as nothing more than bare life, something monstrous that exists between the animal and the human.

This act of banning is also a very useful way of understanding what Agamben means by 'inclusive exclusion', and I shall return to it in Chapter Two. From the position of the bandit, that is from the position of bare life, to be banned is to be abandoned by sovereign power. In this sense the bandit is excluded or banned from social space. However, the Old English word 'ban' means 'to call for by public proclamation' and it has since taken the meaning of banning as exclusion. What this indicates is that to be banned is first to be marked by sovereign power and then to be excluded. In the act of banning the bandit bears the mark of sovereign power, and is completely exposed to sovereign power at the same time as he is excluded. This is what Agamben means by 'inclusive exclusion'. Bare life is created in an act of power that includes us within the space of power, at the same time, it seems to exclude us from all protection. We can see quite clearly how the exposure to death is then an act of power that creates a life that is always threatened by death.

Like the sacred man the bandit is a marginal figure. How can Agamben go on to claim, as he does, that bare life is central to the political order and especially central in modern culture? Today, Agamben will say, we all share the fate of the sacred man and we are all left exposed to death by power. This is what he calls the thanatopolitics of modernity. The situation of being left exposed to death can explain what Norman Mailer suggested: that life today is lived under the constant threat of death, from beginning to end and that the 'end' loses its sense of finality and meaning. What is peculiar about the modern culture of death is that the dividing line between life and death is particularly unstable. We live in a 'zone of indistinction' between life and death, as Agamben puts it. He explains this situation as being the result of the sacred man moving from the margins of our culture to the centre. Disturbingly, according to Agamben, this is the result of the rise of democracy in the West. Democracy began as a challenge to the powers of the sovereign; however, ironically, it would not put an end to sovereign power but instead offered 'a new and more dreadful foundation' for sovereign power (HS: 121).

Why is this? Those who called for democracy attacked the sovereign in the name of political rights, such as the 'rights of man'. However, these rights were founded in the body defined as a political body. The writers of the American Declaration of Independence (1776) stated that 'We hold these truths to be self-evident, that all men are created equal, that they are endowed by their Creator with certain unalienable Rights, that among these are Life, Liberty and the pursuit of Happiness.' This text links together rights with the body ('life') and its needs ('liberty and the pursuit of happiness'). In this way politics still remains centred on bare life, but now bare life belongs to all as the foundation of their political identity. So the rights of man are founded on bare life but what is ignored is that it is bare life where sovereign power exercises its authority. Therefore the space of liberation turns back into the space of subjection to power and subjection to the threat of death.

Let us consider one of the founding democratic rights, the 1679 writ of *habeas corpus*. This writ is supposed to limit the power of the sovereign to detain a person without trial, and today this right is being eroded in the 'war against terrorism', when suspects are being held without trial. However, what interests Agamben is the fact that this right is founded on the rights of the body. In this way political identity is no longer defined in political terms but is defined through the biological body. Politics is, more and more, a politics of the body and of life: biopolitics. The body forms the new basis for political identity and so bare life comes to stand at the centre of political life and our culture. As Agamben puts it, 'modern democracy does not abolish sacred life but rather shatters it and disseminates it into every individual body, making it into what is at stake in political conflict' (HS: 124). The result then is that now we are all *homo sacer*. Our exposure to the threat of death from sovereign power has not been reduced by the rise of democracy but extended. Here Agamben offers us a useful means for understanding why modern death might involve further exposure to death rather than death simply becoming taboo.

Although both the sacred man and the bandit were marginal figures the rise of democracy has placed bare life as the central concept of the modern political order. Of course, for Agamben, Western culture has always been about defining bare life, and so life and death have always been political concepts. In this sense there is a strong continuity within the Western culture of death. What happens today, though, is that this political definition of death has extended itself across the whole of our politics and the whole of our culture. Now, entire populations, and not just individuals or groups of individuals, become subject to the fate of abandonment and the threat of death. The new contemporary interest in the body, which ranges across sociology, history, philosophy, feminism and art, might well be a symptom of this modern exposure of the body to death. If the body is central to modern political systems then it should come as no surprise that the body has also become central to contemporary academic thought.

However, all too often the academic study of the body ignores the fact that the body is the site of our exposure to death. Instead it often celebrates the body as the place where when can discover a new foundation for our politics or for new ways of thinking and writing. It fails to consider how the body is captured and fragmented by power into the residue of bare life exposed to death. T. S. Eliot's poem 'The Waste Land' (1922) offers a more pessimistic interpretation of this situation: 'A crowd flowed over London Bridge, so many, / I had not thought death had undone so many' (1963: 65). In these lines 'death' is not the exterior ending of life but something that inhabits the bodies of those in the urban crowd, leaving them already 'undone'. Of course for Eliot this 'death' is more spiritual than physical, and he is referring in these lines to Dante's *Inferno*. However, it could be that this urban 'hell' is also the hell of the work of death in modern culture. It is mass death which affects the 'crowd' that flows across London Bridge. Also, it is death that acts on these individuals although they are still alive; it is death as a living death. These two factors, its mass anonymity and the fact it acts on the 'living', suggest something of our exposure to death as bare life. Certainly Eliot is writing of a spiritual death but his work also indicates something of our exposure to death in modern democratic societies.

One obvious issue with this argument is the hostility that Agamben seems to have for modern democracy. If he is so critical of democracy, is he calling for a return to non-democratic political systems? Agamben rejects the charge that he is demanding any return to the supposed certainties of Ancient

Greece or Rome, or to some new anti-democratic political system. Instead we must face the fact that the founding rights of modern democracy come with a political cost: they are based on the body that is exposed to death. This means that we must take a critical approach to modern democracy and not simply accept that it is the best, or least worst, political system. Agamben therefore belongs with a small number of other contemporary philosophers who are openly critical of democracy. He is critical of the fact it rests on the concept of bare life without recognising this and its effects. Further, he argues that this dependence on bare life means that it much harder to distinguish between democratic states and totalitarian states. The fact that, during the period from the 1930s to the end of the Second World War, states like Germany went from being democracies to becoming totalitarian states and then back to being democracies with such speed indicates, for Agamben, that in both types of state 'biological life and its needs had become the *politically* decisive fact' (HS: 122).

Agamben is very critical of the direction in which the contemporary democracies of the West are moving as well. He suggests we are witnessing the emergence of post-democratic spectacular societies in which democracy is no longer a matter of the ballot box but more of the opinion poll, the spin-doctor and advertising. Perhaps this fear is not surprising as Agamben is Italian. In contemporary Italy the Prime Minister Silvio Berlusconi carefully cultivates his image, has control over his own TV network, as well as many other businesses, and also happens to be Italy's richest man. He is the prototype of a new type of media monopolist politician and close friends with both the American president George Bush and the British Prime Minister Tony Blair. For Agamben this sort of state is at risk of combining a watered-down democracy with some of the 'old' features of totalitarian states: media manipulation, cult of personality and the endemic corruption of the political process. Perhaps we need this warning about the dangers of the transformation of democracy especially in the wake of the legislation introduced in the United States, Britain and other Western countries as a result of the 'war against terrorism'.

Recently Giorgio Agamben himself has refused to enter the United States due to the new legislation demanding the photographing and fingerprinting of foreign visitors (Schaefer, 2003). As an Italian citizen Agamben is exempt from these procedures, but he has expressed his solidarity with those who are not because of his concern with this new form of political registration. He sees this process of registration as a kind of biopolitical tattooing, which sets a dangerous precedent for what we might accept as the 'normal' registration of our identity as a citizen. It seems that contemporary events are intent on confirming Agamben's diagnosis about the risks of democracy and the dangers of a political identity that is founded on the body. This biopolitical registration is another example of the process by which we have moved from a distinctly separate figure of bare life, the sacred man, to one in which each of us plays this role. As he puts it, 'If today there is no longer any one clear figure of the sacred man, it is perhaps because we are all virtually *homines sacri*' (HS: 115).

His thesis is also useful in explaining why we might be entering a new modern culture of death. Although he stresses that Western culture has always been founded on the definition of bare life, today, he argues, bare life has spread across our culture. If bare life is life exposed to death then this means that we will experience our exposure to death in new ways in modern culture. One sign of this is in contemporary literature. For example, the American novelist Don DeLillo's *White Noise* (1985) is a novel that is fascinated with death and our exposure to death. DeLillo (b. 1936) says that 'It's about fear, death, and technology. A comedy, of course.' The novel concerns an academic, Jack Gladney, and his family, who may, or may not, be exposed to contamination by the Airborne Toxic Event. The reason for the uncertainty is that it is never clear whether this event exists or whether it is the result of media panic. However, Gladney and many of the other characters in the book display an obsessive fear of death, and especially of the exposure and contamination of modern death as a result of the 'white noise' of modern technology. While the novel reflects on the idea that death is taboo, and therefore more and more terrifying, it also explores our exposure to death, whether through toxic waste spills, air crashes, or our culture's obsession with violence (Gladney is a professor of 'Hitler Studies'). Is this the best way in which we can understand our exposure to death in modern culture?

AGAMBEN VERSUS BAUDRILLARD

We can usefully compare Agamben's claims about our exposure to death with a rival argument made by the French social theorist Jean Baudrillard. Baudrillard is best known for his discussion of contemporary society as a society of simulation, in which the real is replaced by images to produce the hyperreal.[2] For example, the reality of the Vietnam War is replaced by the simulation of that war in Francis Ford Coppola's film *Apocalypse Now* (1979), to the point where any distinction between the 'actual' war and its simulation threatens to disappear (Baudrillard, 1994: 59–60). Although Baudrillard is often seen as celebrating this new 'postmodern' situation where images dominate reality, he is, in fact, critical of this loss of the real. In particular he has been critical of our loss of the sense of the reality of death. His book *Symbolic Exchange and Death* (1993 [1976]) claims that contemporary Western culture rests on the exclusion of death and the dead from society, but also that death cannot be excluded and that it threatens to undermine our postmodern culture of images. Although Baudrillard's theory of death has often been dismissed, his extreme position is useful for allowing us a comparison with Agamben because it is also a theory about our exposure to death in modern culture.

What Baudrillard stresses is that although modern culture tries to exclude death it fails. Today the dead are not included within the space of the city, either in charnel-houses or in cemeteries attached to churches, but are excluded by being placed in mass cemeteries which lie outside the city. However, the more our culture tries to push the reality of death away, the more it tries to isolate the dead, the more death threatens to invade our whole culture. Baudrillard can then agree with the idea that death has become taboo but also argue that this process has failed and that it leaves us more exposed to death. How does this take place? For Baudrillard so-called 'primitive' cultures used to organise symbolic exchange with the dead, regarding them in some sense as present, but today we try not to deal with the dead at all. The result is that 'we trade with our dead in a kind of melancholy, while the primitives live with their dead under the auspices of the ritual and the feast' (Baudrillard, 1993: 135). What has caused this is the decline and eclipse of symbolic exchange due to the rise of capitalism.

Capitalism is organised around market exchanges in which goods are exchanged through the medium of money. The emphasis is often on the fairness of exchange, on the idea that the market-place adjusts prices through competition, and on anonymous exchange where the producers of goods and their consumers are separated in space and time. What has been lost in this market-based exchange is the idea of symbolic exchange. This is a form of exchange which is not based on getting something equal in return for what we spend but exchange as an unbalanced and excessive social process. The classic example of symbolic exchange is that of gift-giving, in particular the Native American practice of potlatch. The word is from the Chinook language and means 'to give'. It is the name for a ceremonial feast of north-west coast tribes at which the host distributed his possessions as gifts to his guests. These gifts could be material things like blankets and furniture, but also food, and they would win honour for the host. What interested anthropologists in this gift-giving was that it could also seemingly run out of control, with whole villages being made destitute in trying to provide gifts. Capitalism replaces this form of exchange, which is based on social prestige and direct personal relationships, with forms of exchange based on calculation and the anonymity of the market. For Baudrillard this eclipse of symbolic exchange also affected our relationship with death.

As symbolic exchange is destroyed, including our exchanges with the dead, so 'little by little, *the dead cease to exist*' (Baudrillard, 1993: 126). Once we had exchanges with the dead, we traded or bargained with them, or made offerings to them. This extends to practices like the Irish wake, when a party would be held while the body of the dead was still in the house to celebrate the life of the deceased. Now, the dead are excluded, we remove them as rapidly as possible to be buried or cremated and mourning rituals have also been curtailed. Baudrillard argues that we can never completely eliminate symbolic exchange or our dealings with the dead. The more we try to exclude the dead the more they return in traumatic forms. Perhaps the modern fashion for zombie films, such as the trilogy of George A. Romero, *Night of the Living Dead* (1969), *Dawn of the Dead* (1979) and *Day of the Dead* (1985), is a sign of this? What is interesting is that in the second film of the trilogy, *Dawn of the Dead*, the zombies invade that bastion of capitalist culture the shopping mall (although they seem strangely pacified by the muzak!).

What is also interesting is that this film is the one from the trilogy that has recently been remade.

In a sense death takes its revenge on us as, for Baudrillard, death can never be fully programmed or contained by the postmodern society of images. The dead resist the process of exchange and cannot be fully integrated into the capitalist economy. This is despite the fact that, as Nancy Mitford pointed out in her 1963 book *The American Way of Death* (1998), a scathing exposé of funeral home practices, there is a great deal of money to be made in the funeral business. Baudrillard emphasised that this return of the dead would force us to rediscover symbolic exchange or we would be left with a culture that had become terminal. Either we deal with the dead through symbolic exchange, or we become the living dead, like the zombie consumers of *Dawn of the Dead*. His work is almost a parody of those radical thinkers of the 1960s who tried to find resistance in those who could not be integrated into the system, whether that was women, students, lesbians and gays, petty criminals or African-Americans. It seems as if, for Baudrillard, the dead are the only ones who cannot be integrated!

The problem with his model is that it offers no real explanation for why death comes to invade our whole culture. His idea of a radical reversal, when what is excluded returns in a more virulent form, is extremely hard to pin down concretely. This leaves his argument ungrounded and it is no surprise that it has been greeted with scepticism. In comparison, whatever criticisms we might want to make of it, Agamben's analysis of our exposure to death is more concretely grounded. The increasing exposure to death in modern culture is understood as the result of the act of sovereign power that creates bare life, a life exposed to death. In modern culture this production of bare life has spread because bare life has become the ground of our political identity. Agamben does not regard death as some point of resistance that somehow lies outside our culture. In treating death as a point of resistance Baudrillard is in danger of turning death into some sort of authentic experience where we can find, or recover, our true values. In fact, the exposure to death in modern culture seems to be, as we shall see later in this book, a far more banal and everyday process.

Baudrillard's model does explore our exposure to death in modern culture but it seems to offer no adequate explanation for that exposure. Instead it offers something like a magical or metaphysical thinking where what is excluded can only ever return in a more extreme form. Agamben provides an analysis which is more precise but which is also not beyond criticism. If Baudrillard's thesis has proven controversial and been treated with scepticism then so have Agamben's claims. In particular, his history of bare life has faced five major criticisms. The first is that Agamben's theory concerning bare life is not well supported by the historical evidence and that he is selective in the evidence he draws on. Secondly, that Agamben's history of bare life is too straightforward, too linear, and so doesn't really deal with the complex nature of the social history of death. Thirdly, that in only studying Western culture Agamben is ethnocentric, and that he excludes evidence from other cultures and tends to treat Western culture as a monolithic whole. Fourthly, that Agamben's model of biopolitics tends to erase the important distinctions between different political systems, especially between democracies and totalitarian states. And, finally, that he does not consider in enough depth the different experiences of exposure to death, or the fact that this exposure to death is unevenly distributed.

CRITICISMS OF AGAMBEN

1. Agamben's history of bare life is very rapidly undertaken and is not supported by a wide range of historical evidence. One exasperated critic has argued that this history is 'fabulous' and often 'close to fanciful' (Fitzpatrick, 2001: 259). Certainly it makes large historical leaps, from Ancient Roman law to the Middle Ages, from the birth of modern democracy to the concentration camps. At each point it asserts a continuity of the existence of the sacred man but how can we be sure we are dealing with the same figure in new guises? Could Agamben's history be seen as a kind of myth of the culture of death, or even a fable? Certainly a great deal more historical research would be required to substantiate his theory, and it is disappointing how little he considers the wider literature of death studies. His proposals must be considered as more tentative hypotheses than his style sometimes suggests. What is valuable about his theory, though, is the way it allows us

to start to consider the issue of our exposure to death, both in the past and in modern culture. What is also useful is how this very partial history draws our attention to how issues in the present, such as the erosion of democratic values and the new measures of the war against terrorism, might be shaped by the history of our political concepts.

2. Agamben's history of bare life also tells us a remarkably straightforward story about Western culture. We begin with the distinction between bare life and political life in Ancient Greece. In Roman law bare life is confined to the sacred man and then the sacred man becomes the key figure of our history. What happens in modern culture is the loss of the distinction so that political life is bare life; our political identity is founded on our exposure to death. This is what Agamben calls the 'zone of indistinction'. Although Agamben emphasises this indistinction he actually gives us a very clear picture of the history of bare life. In particular, this history supposes that we move from an experience of a clear division between political life and biological life to a more blurred situation. Yet it may be that what Edgar Allan Poe described as the shadowy border between life and death has always been indistinct, or more indistinct then Agamben realises. On the other hand, the usefulness of this history is that it draws attention to certain features of modern culture but, once again, these need to be closely examined to see if there really is a modern culture of death.

3. The story that Agamben tells is an explicitly Western story, concerned only with the West, from Ancient Greece to modernity. This means that he largely ignores the rich anthropological discourse on death; nor does he consider other 'non-Western' ways of dying. Also, Agamben often contends that the problem of bare life is a global one without exploring how this globalisation of bare life might be taking place. He does not engage with any work in postcolonial studies that examines how the history of colonialism has also involved the history of defining and controlling bodies. However, his emphasis on the West could be justified, as I have suggested, in terms of the fact that Western culture is imposing itself globally, even if Agamben is largely silent on the precise mechanisms by which this is happening.

4. Another problem with the 'zone of indistinction' is the indistinction it produces between democratic and totalitarian states. The result seems to be a collapsing of differences between these forms of state, to the point

where they are equally criticised for the failure to come to terms with bare life. Although democracy is preferable to the totalitarian state it still condemns us to an existence of 'perfect senselessness' (HS: 11). While this is problematic, as we have seen Agamben is alerting us to the dangers of democracy, especially when complacently treated as the best of political forms. He is challenging us to consider whether our current forms of democracy are really democratic and whether they allow us to come to terms with our exposure as bare life. This might be uncomfortable to think, and even dangerous in political terms, but perhaps no more dangerous than the degeneration of democracy, with declining voter interest and the dominance of the image in politics.

5. The final problem is that of the distribution of our vulnerability or exposure to death. Agamben declares that we are all virtually sacred men but nowhere has he considered how differently that exposure is experienced. As we might argue that bare life is far more exposed in totalitarian states than in democratic states, or, at least, has fewer legal, political, social or cultural possibilities of resisting power, so we might want to examine in far more detail the questions: 'Who is exposed to death?' and 'How are they are exposed to death?' Modern death may be a virtual threat hanging over everyone, but is also a more precise and real threat to certain subjects left radically exposed as bare life. Today, it is not only certain figures that are highly exposed as bare life (AIDS sufferers, 'terrorist' suspects, asylum seekers) but even countries (Iraq?) and whole continents ('Africa'). A more differentiated account of bare life, and of power, would allow a better understanding of this uneven distribution of the exposure of bare life.

CONCLUSION: THE QUESTION OF MODERN DEATH

Agamben is not, obviously, unaware of these difficulties and his work closely tracks different forms and figures of bare life. His work also, currently, remains incomplete. However, even when it is completed it remains doubtful whether it will address all the points of weakness that I have raised. What remains important is that his intervention is an unprecedented attempt to account for modern death and to put into question the ground of life on which so many of the investigations of death uncritically turn. In particular, Agamben will allow us to deepen our understanding of death in relation to power. Already it should be evident that Agamben challenges many of the contemporary understandings of the culture of death. He brings into focus the zone of indistinction that seems to surround the time of death in modern culture in a precise fashion. In doing so he allows us to grasp the dimensions of horror and banality provoked by modern death without lapsing into the sort of metaphysics of death we found in Baudrillard.

What is important is to explore his arguments further and to place them in a more detailed dialogue with other approaches to death. This will involve trying to rectify some of the faults of his account and taking it further, while at the same time treating it critically. We must begin to grasp the nature of our exposure to death in modern culture and to assess how far this exposure has really altered. To do so will involve us visiting some of the spaces of modern death, from the hospital room to the site of the car accident. In particular what will prove of value in Agamben's work is his stress on the decision on the time of death as a political decision. This will allow us to think about and challenge the politics of death and, in particular, the politics of modern death or what Agamben calls 'thanatopolitics'.

NOTES

1. The original Italian *vita nuda* can be translated as either bare life or naked life. I will use the translation 'bare life' except when quoting from works which use the alternative.
2. The best introductory book on Baudrillard's work is Rex Butler's *Jean Baudrillard: The Defence of the Real* (1999).

CHAPTER 2

The Space of Death

INTRODUCTION: THE OLD POWER OF DEATH

Now we must begin to examine the spaces in modern culture where the decision on the time of death takes place and to examine these spaces as spaces of power. For Agamben, the power over life and death is sovereign power, and sovereign power is exercised through a particular form of space. It is in this form of space that power constructs bare life. Traditionally, sovereign power has been seen as the power of the head of state, and it includes the power over life and death. Agamben suggests that sovereign power is not the possession of the sovereign, or any individual, but a space of power in which bare life is produced. In returning to sovereign power Agamben is returning to the old power of death. For many contemporary theorists power can no longer be understood through the concept of sovereignty. They stress that power today is plural, dispersed and fragmented and also no longer focused on death. Agamben argues against this view, and he allows us to see that when we talk about power we are also talking about death. Also, he offers some provocative suggestions about the nature of power today and why we are still living within a culture of death.

The most insistent critic of the idea of sovereign power, and the critic who has had most influence on models of power in contemporary sociology and cultural studies, is Michel Foucault (1926–1984). He is well known for his historical studies of institutions such as the asylum, the clinic and the prison, as well as for his multi-volume history of sexuality. In the first volume of that history of sexuality he also offered a new formulation of the nature of power, writing that 'Power is everywhere; not because it embraces everything but because it comes from everywhere' (Foucault, 1979a: 93).

This challenged the idea that power was the possession of an individual, of the state or of a particular class (such as the working class). It also consigned the idea of sovereign power to the past, as he suggested that this new model of power which was focused on life had replaced the old power of death. What is odd is that Agamben sees his work as continuing Foucault's enquiry into power, although he comes to very different conclusions.

The debate between Agamben and Foucault will offer us a staging of what is at stake in the relationship of power to death, and a reflection on the problems with models that regard power as plural and fragmented. Agamben argues that Foucault's work requires correction because of two significant failings. The first is that Foucault cannot explain the connection of power to bodies, despite the fact that Foucault sets out to 'show how deployments of power are directly connected to the body – to bodies, functions, physiological processes, sensations, and pleasures' (1979a: 151–2). Foucault's second failing is that he does not consider the places in which modern power exposes life to death: the concentration camps and the extermination camps (HS: 4). To correct both these failings requires us to return to sovereignty as the old power of death, which may not be so old but actually the form of modern power.

Agamben and Foucault have opposed understandings of the relationship between power and death. While Agamben sees power as always a power of death and, in its essence, a political power of death – thanatopolitical – in contrast Foucault sees death as the limit of power. As he writes in Volume 1 of *The History of Sexuality*, 'death is power's limit, the moment that escapes it; death becomes the most secret aspect of existence, the most "private"' (1979a: 138). Foucault is another example of the tendency to see modern death as invisible or taboo. In lectures given while he was conducting his research on power and sexuality Foucault stated that '[Death] has become the most private and shameful thing of all (and ultimately, it is not so much sex as death that is the object of a taboo)' (2003: 247). This model of death as taboo is highly problematic, and Agamben contends that the old power of death has not disappeared in modern culture but taken new, more virulent forms.

This virulence is most visible in the space of the camp. There the inmates are exposed to death at every turn, and power does not find its limit in death but extends itself into death. While Foucault examined many different spaces of power in modern culture he never examined the concentration or extermination camps. Instead he disputed the idea that there was any one privileged space of power. Just as there are multiple relations of power so there are multiple spaces of power. Agamben sees things very differently: the camp 'is the fundamental biopolitical paradigm of the West' (HS: 181). His argument appears to be supported by the re-emergence of the concentration camp during the war in the former Yugoslavia and in new forms of detention 'camp' since then. However, it is also highly controversial, especially with his claim that the camps are not simply places where death is mass-produced but places for the production of bare life reduced to pure survival. The risk, which I shall explore later in this chapter, is that Agamben will lose sight of the specificity of the Holocaust and suggest that many radically different types of camp share the same form.

Another risk is that his claim that the Nazi camps aimed at producing bare life ignores the fact that the 'final solution' was a project of extermination. It also ignores the role of the ideology of racism that intended the destruction of 'racial' groups, primarily the Jews, in the Holocaust. No study of death in modern culture can ignore the implications of the Holocaust. However, to understand these implications requires that we try to grasp what happened during the Holocaust as precisely as possible. Despite his denials, Agamben is in danger of ignoring this need and replacing a close analysis with an argument that does not properly take into account what happened during the Holocaust. Although he may help us to correct some strange absences in Foucault's works, absences that are often repeated in death studies, his work must be approached critically. To do this we must examine his arguments about power and his dispute with Foucault in some detail.

THE SPACE OF SOVEREIGNTY

First, what is the space of sovereignty that Agamben describes? The usual understanding of the power of sovereignty is that it is the power to decide when a legal and political order has entered a time when it must be suspended. This is the 'state of exception': for example, when a state of emergency or martial law is declared. Agamben approaches sovereignty in a different way; although he sees it as an act of decision he does not see it as the expression of the will of a particular sovereign. Instead, sovereignty is the matter of power taking up bare life and including it within power (HS: 25–6). It is not the act of a subject, typically the head of state, or the possession of an individual, such as the sovereign. Instead, sovereignty is a space of power in which sovereign power produces bare life through, as we saw in Chapter One, 'inclusive exclusion'.

What is the spatial structure of sovereignty? In *Homo Sacer* Agamben tries to reconstruct this spatial structure and provide what he calls a topology of sovereignty. Topology is the mathematical discipline that studies the properties of geometric figures that remain unchanged even when under distortion. What Agamben is studying are the unchanging properties of the space of sovereignty, despite the distortions this space of power undergoes. This is a complex topology because sovereignty occupies a paradoxical position as simultaneously both inside and outside the legal and political order. On the one hand, it is at the very heart of the legal and political order as the function that can place that order in suspension. However, on the other hand, to suspend the legal and political order it has to remain, in a sense, outside that order. Agamben explains the paradoxical position of sovereignty by considering it as a particular form of relation: the relation of exception. This relation of exception is a limit-relation that is at the edge of what we normally consider the operation of relation. If a relation is usually a connection between things, the relation of exception is a relation that connects sovereignty to bare life by abandoning bare life.

Not only does sovereignty decide on the state or relation of exception but it also exists as a state of exception. Sovereignty remains in a relation of exception to the legal and political order as the exceptional moment that allows that order to be suspended. It is in the paradoxical position of both declaring the state of exception and existing as a state of exception. This means it belongs to the relation of exception and so is 'outside' the legal and political order but also what determines what is 'outside' that order. This 'outside' is not the result of an act of exclusion or of the inclusion of what is pushed outside. Power, and we must remember this is power over bare life, does not work by either interdiction or internment. It does not confine within itself what it defines as the 'outside' (criminals, perverts, the mentally ill, etc.), nor does it simply operate by the act of exclusion. So, contrary to Baudrillard's argument discussed in Chapter One, death is not excluded in modern culture.

Instead, sovereign power works through the act of suspension, and this is how it creates bare life as life exposed to death. In this suspension what is left as the exception, that is, bare life, is left abandoned by the law but still left in relation to the law. We can describe this relation of exception in which the law is suspended as inclusive exclusion. In Chapter One we saw how bare life is subject to this relation by being left by power in the position of inclusive exclusion. Bare life is included and so exposed radically to power and the threat of death, but only by being excluded, that is, abandoned. This is the double movement of power that combines the act of inclusion with the act of exclusion. At the same time as this act of sovereign power sets bare life apart, it also draws bare life within itself. The result is that sovereign power is the uncanny double of bare life, as both exist as exceptional states, the one determined by the other. They both exist as the two limits of the space of power, on one side sovereign power and on the other side bare life.

Already we can see how the relation of exception might begin to answer the problem of the connection of power to bodies that Foucault left unaccounted for. This 'connection', though, is not any common sort of relation but at the very limit of relation. Contrary to what Foucault stated, power does not simply connect directly to bodies in some unspecified way. Instead, the relationship that forms between power and bodies is a relation that operates through leaving bare life abandoned. In abandoning bare life, leaving it excluded, sovereign power also includes it within the space of power. At the same time it also exposes it to death, so that death is not power's limit but the terrain on which it operates. To understand exactly how this strange 'relation' of power to bodies works, we can return to the example of the ban that I discussed in Chapter One: this time to explore how the ban operates from the position of power, rather than from the position of bare life.

We saw how the ban placed the bandit in the position of bare life, leaving the bandit exposed to the threat of death and exposed to power. However, the ban can be understood in a more general way as the space of sovereign power. Agamben is always interested in the properties of sovereignty that remain unchanged despite the distortions of its space. Therefore, the ban is not simply one relation of exception during one particular historical period but a key form of the relation of exception that remains constant. As Agamben writes, 'the relation of ban has constituted the essential structure of sovereign power from the beginning' (HS: 111). What the ban will demonstrate is that power does not work by directly connecting to bodies; instead it works indirectly by creating a space in which bodies are abandoned by power. This will allow Agamben to answer the question: how does power connect to bodies? It will also allow him to insist that this question is always a matter of life and death because it is always about the production of bare life.

KAFKA AND THE BAN

To explain this further I want to turn to an example that, for Agamben, is the best short summary of the sovereign space as the space of the ban. This can be found in the work of the Jewish modernist writer Franz Kafka (1883–1924). Kafka created some of the most disturbing literary works ever written. Agamben's example is taken from his second novel, *The Trial* (1925), in which Josef K. in arrested, tried and finally executed, for a crime that is never specified. The novel includes a parable, 'Before the Law', which is told to Josef K. by a priest. This parable gives us the description of the nature of the ban. In it a man from the country asks for entry into the law but finds his way barred by a door-keeper. The door-keeper explains that it is possible to enter the law but not at the moment. He also explains that should the man from the country be tempted to try and enter he will stop him. Even though he is only the lowliest of the door-keepers he is still powerful, and the man from the country will have to face the others if he gets past him. The man from the country waits before the door for days and then years, asking questions, begging admission and even attempting to bribe the door-keeper, all to no avail. Finally his eyes grow weak and he realises that he is dying, he summons the strength to ask one last question, 'How is it that in all these years nobody except myself has asked for admittance?'

(Kafka, 2000: 167). The door-keeper knows the man is near death and so replies, 'Nobody else could gain admittance here, this entrance was meant only for you. I shall now go and close it' (2000: 167).

According to Agamben the man from the country is in the position of bare life, left before the law but banned from entering it. This relationship to the law represents the law suspended in the state of exception; there is no law to actually enter because it is not in proper operation. We can see this because, although the man from the country is barred from entry, the door of the law is left open. The open door of the law is the sign that the law is suspended, and so both available and unavailable at the same time. When the man from the country is dying and his eyes grow dim he can even see a glowing light shining from this open door. How then does the law position the man from the country? He is left in the position of inclusive exclusion: excluded because he cannot enter the door of the law until too late but included because he remains perpetually before the law. We can even see how he is produced as bare life when he becomes progressively feebler and is finally exposed to death.

Kafka is often seen as the prophet of the alienation of modern life and of the power of inhumane bureaucracies to determine our fate. However, somewhat ironically, Agamben regards this Kafka parable as offering us hope. Why is this? The final act of the door-keeper in closing the door of the law might seem to be the end of any hope for the man from the country. Instead, Agamben suggests that this closing of the door of the law might indicate that the suspension of the law is being brought to an end. When the door is closed the man from the country is not simply left permanently excluded from the law but his vigil before the law finally comes to an end. This means that if we wish to escape the space of power then, somehow, we must bring to an end the relation of the ban that leaves us before the law that never exists except by being suspended. As we shall see in Chapter Six, Agamben finds hope in the most desperate of situations, and the hope here is that we might be able to finally end our being left before the law.

The importance of the Kafka example is that this strange parable describes the space of sovereign power as the space of the ban. When we consider the man from the country we can see that he is banned from entering the law but that this ban does not simply leave him outside the law. Instead of being outside the law he is perpetually before it, held by the law, by the power of the door-keeper and the fascination of the mysterious glow from the door of the law. As bare life we are in the same position, included before the law but excluded from entering into it. We can see how this is still a space of power, where power does not directly connect to bodies but holds us fast by leaving us outside itself. If this is the nature of sovereign power then how can Agamben respond to Foucault's criticism that sovereignty is the 'old power' that has been superseded in modern culture?

FOUCAULT AND THE END OF SOVEREIGNTY

Foucault completely rejects the model of sovereign power; he argues that 'the representation of power has remained under the spell of monarchy. In political thought and analysis, we still have not cut off the head of the king' (1979a: 88–9). This failure to 'cut off the head of the king' means that we have not properly grasped the actual mechanisms of modern power. Instead of trying to describe the sovereign as the individual who possesses power, we should turn to the concrete analysis of 'how multiple bodies, forces, energies, matters, desires, thoughts, and so on are gradually, progressively, actually and materially constituted as subjects, or as the subject' (Foucault, 2003: 28). This is the new approach to power that has dominated sociology and cultural studies, which have often turned away from the idea of power as contained within an individual or group. Instead, they have examined the processes by which individuals are transformed into subjects of power in particular historical and cultural contexts.

In fact, Foucault regards any analysis that is still fascinated with sovereign power as trapped in the past. It is in danger of being obsessed with a form of power that has passed away: the old power of death. Power today is not about the relationship between the sovereign and his or her subjects but about the multiple effects of power that constitute different types of subject. These new forms of power are molecular and local; they do not exist in one space of power but range across different spaces of power, each with their own unique features. Foucault is not interested in providing a new model of power for the sake of it, but he sees these new forms of power as the result of a historical mutation in regimes of power. Beginning in the eighteenth century, power shifts away from the sovereign and his power to inflict death. A new regime of power arises, which exists across the social field and is focused on life. These new molecular power relations are the result of power taking 'charge of men's existence, men as living bodies' (Foucault, 1979a: 89). As power does so, it reflects the diverse, unstable and molecular nature of life. This is the rise of what Foucault calls biopolitics: a new politics of life.

The time of sovereignty is over and in modern culture 'the ancient right to *take* life or *let* live [is] replaced by a power to *foster* life or *disallow* it to the point of death' (Foucault, 1979a: 138). Sovereign power was a power that was active when it inflicted death, and if it were not active then it would 'let live'. Modern power is a power over life, biopolitics or biopower, which is active when it fosters life. It makes us live and lets us die. If sovereign power exposed us to death then modern power sets out to 'invest life through and through' (Foucault, 1979a: 139). This is why, for Foucault, death is the limit of modern power. It is the point where modern power can no longer take hold and apply itself. In this way his argument converges with Baudrillard's claim that death is somehow outside, or resistant to, modern power.

This shift from sovereign power to modern power is most memorably presented in the opening of Foucault's book *Discipline and Punish*. It begins with the detailed description of the terrible punishment undergone by Damien the regicide, tortured and then pulled apart by horses. Here sovereign power faces the body of the criminal in an excessive theatre of torture and death. Power, as in Kafka's short story 'In the Penal Colony', literally inscribes the crime on the suffering body of the convicted criminal. Then Foucault makes a rapid shift to prison regulations where the criminal is subject to a minute organisation of every aspect of their life (1979b: 3–7). What this jump marks is the change in the regime of power that I have been describing. From the power to inflict death we have passed to the power which invests life through and through by regulating every aspect of bodily behaviour. These two scenes summarise the two significant transformations I have sketched: first, from a single relation of power to multiple relations of power; and, secondly, from the sovereign power that operates by making die, executing in this case, to the new biopower that makes us live.

Agamben agrees with Foucault that politics is biopolitics but he argues that this has always been the case. From the beginning, sovereign power has been the power over both life and death, over bare life where we find life defined as the exposure to death. What happens in modern culture is that this link between power and life becomes more explicit. Where once it only seemed to apply to marginal cases, such as the sacred man or the bandit, now it more clearly applies to all political identities. Also, Agamben argues that we have not witnessed the end of sovereignty with the rise of modern biopolitics. In fact, sovereignty has extended itself and spread throughout modern culture. While Foucault argues that power has become dispersed into multiple power relations exercised over life and bodies, Agamben argues that sovereignty remains as the space of power but one that can no longer be localised. This is what he calls the 'zone of indistinction'.[1]

It is through the concept of the 'zone of indistinction' that Agamben can account for what appears to be the fragmentation of power in modern culture while, at the same time, stressing its fundamental unity in the space of sovereign power. In Chapter One we saw how bare life moves from the margins of Western culture to occupy the central position as the direct foundation of all political identity. As it does so, then so sovereign power becomes more and more central as well. However, as bare life spreads into every political identity so the space of sovereign power becomes indistinct, and not simply fragmented. So, contrary to Foucault, we do not have multiple spaces of power but we have one fundamental space of power that has become indistinct because it is no longer located securely in one figure (if, of course, it ever was). Instead of this being the end of sovereign power it is actually a sign of the dispersal of sovereign power throughout the social body. What remains is the space of sovereignty but it is no longer stable or secure.

This is what Agamben also calls the 'state of emergency'. As we have seen, sovereign power operates by suspending the law, by declaring a state of emergency. This does not merely mean that power withdraws but that as it withdraws it can operate with impunity. States of emergency are states when the normal operation of the law is suspended and new more extreme operations of power are permitted. If sovereign power has spread across our culture then what has also spread is the state of emergency. No longer is this state exceptional but the exception has become permanent. Therefore we live in a state of permanent emergency, and this has recently become visible with the new regulations that have emerged during the 'war against terrorism' and the suspension, or threatened suspension, of democratic rights, such as the right to trial by jury and *habeas corpus*. In the same way that bare life was once marginal and is now the norm, so too sovereign power has become the norm of power and so too has the state of emergency. If modern culture has entered the zone of indistinction then in this zone we are far more exposed and vulnerable to power, and so to death, than we have been previously.

Therefore Agamben links together Foucault's enquiries on biopolitics with his own work on sovereignty to argue that power leaves us completely exposed to death, and that this exposure is 'built in' to political identity today. Does Foucault discard the concept of sovereignty completely, as his pronouncements sometimes suggest and as Agamben claims? In fact, his thinking is more nuanced on the point than Agamben recognises. In Volume I of *The History of Sexuality*, Foucault accepts that sovereign power still has a place even if it is 'no longer the major form of power but merely one element among others' (1979a: 136). Yet sovereign power is altered by the rise of biopower so that it is no longer the power to 'make die' but 'a power bent on generating forces, making them grow, and ordering them, rather than one dedicated to impeding them, making them submit, or destroying them' (Foucault, 1979a: 136). Sovereignty may well not have disappeared in Foucault's account but it has been subordinated to a biopower that takes as its object life. What remains obscured in Foucault's model of the space of power is the connection of power to bodies and how power might still be a power to 'let die'.

Foucault leaves death outside of the power relationship. This leaves us with the difficulty of accounting for our exposure to death in modern culture and how this exposure seems to be bound up with the exercise of political power. The most telling, and complex, example is the space of the concentration or extermination camp. In this space we find not only bare life but also power that acts as bare power: ceaselessly and openly inflicting death. What the camps demonstrate is that death is not 'outside the power relationship', nor is it the 'limit of power'. Contrary to Foucault, Agamben might well be inclined to agree with Baudrillard's formulation that 'it is on the manipulation and administration of death that power, in the final analysis, is based' (Baudrillard, 1993: 130). Unlike Baudrillard however, Agamben can provide us with a far more precise model of how power is based 'on the manipulation and administration of death' through his topology of sovereignty. Whereas Baudrillard remains, as we saw, within a metaphysical model of the reversal between the exclusion of death and its violent return, Agamben sets out to explain the exact nature of the relationship between power and death.

The camps disprove Foucault's claim that death is the most secret or private aspect of existence. What the camp produces is not only the space of power peculiar to modern culture but also a space of power where death is no longer either public or private. In the camps the public and the private cannot easily be distinguished. It is a 'private' space as it is self-contained, to an extent, and hidden, to an extent. The historian Raul Hilberg has noted the various methods of concealment that the Nazis used: the speed of the deportations; verbal camouflage (calling the killing centres labour camps (*Arbeitslager*) or concentration camps (*Konzentrationslager*), for example); swearing the most important camp personnel to silence; and control of visitors to the camps (Hilberg, 1985: 240–3). Despite this there were widespread rumours. Also, the camp inhabitant, reduced to pure bare life, has no public existence. But this 'privacy' offers no shelter, because the camp inhabitant is also constantly exposed to power, and is left without any privacy at all. The camp, according to Agamben, is the space of power and the space of the zone of indistinction into which modern power has plunged. What we must now do is assess his analysis of this space to see if it can adequately address this exposure to power and death.

IN THE SPACE OF THE CAMPS

There is already a problem in Agamben's approach due to the imprecision of his terminology and his desire to set out a general model of the structure of 'the camp' as a structure of power. The problem is that this involves a lack of attention to the specific nature of the camps, particularly in the Holocaust. The tendency of Agamben to talk of the camps and concentration camps ignores some very real distinctions, not least between the Nazi concentration camps and the Nazi extermination camps. As the German historian Martin Broszat pointed out in 1962 there is:

> the persistently ignored or denied difference between concentration and extermination camps; the fundamental distinction between the methodical mass murder of millions of Jews in the *extermination* camps in occupied Poland on the one hand, and on the other the individual disposals of *concentration*-camp inmates in Germany – not necessarily, or even primarily Jews – who were no longer useful as workers. (In Sereny, 2000: 137)

The concentration camps were established after the Nazis' rise to power as places to imprison their opponents. They contained, primarily, political prisoners, criminals and some Jews (Hilberg, 1985: 222–3).

Although thousands of inmates were killed in concentration camps – they died of starvation, overwork, due to disease or through execution – these were not death or extermination camps. In contrast, the extermination camps, such as Sobibor or Treblinka, were used for immediate mass killing. As Raul Hilberg writes, 'A man would step off the train in the morning, and in the evening his corpse was burned and his clothes were packed away for shipment to Germany' (Hilberg, 1985: 221). The only inmates used for work purposes were those assigned to the *Sonderkommandos* (special work units), charged with removing valuables from bodies and disposal of the corpses. Agamben's tendency to focus on Auschwitz could be seen as an example of his lack of precision because Auschwitz-Birkenau combined the functions of concentration camp and extermination camp.

Although Agamben sets out to remove these camps from the domain of the unsayable and to explain what juridical and political structures made them possible, his analysis, while suggestive, is not precise enough to deal with the questions raised by the Holocaust. Bearing this profound difficulty in mind, how does Agamben explain the emergence of the concentration camps? His explanation is that the concentration camps are the result of the fragmentation of sovereign power in the zone of indistinction that characterises modern culture. What these camps attempt to do is 'grant the unlocalizable a permanent and visible localization' (HS: 20). What brings about this situation where power faces the unlocalisable element of bare life?

It is the result of the crisis of the modern nation state and especially the crisis of the capacity of the modern nation state to inscribe bare life within a territory and a political order. Between 1915 and 1933 many states, and not only 'totalitarian states', developed new legal measures that deprived groups and individuals of citizenship or denationalised them. Here the state deprives itself of its own power of inscription of bare life and creates a new problem: that of the stateless refugee.

This emergence of mass movements of refugees in Europe left the nation state with the problem of inscribing this new figure of bare life, which was exposed by the state, within the political. The irony is that the state's act of denationalisation of certain citizens left the state incapable of regulating the political inscription of bare life. It is almost as if the state had abandoned bare life to the point where it might escape from power. The camps are a last-ditch attempt to regulate and 'capture' bare life that has lost its inscription into the state, but this capture then takes on a lethal, thanatopolitical, form. So the refugee is bare life created by the space of power but it threatens to dislocate that space of power and turn it into a zone of indistinction. Power attempts to contain this zone of indistinction as a place where it can operate with impunity; the result is the camp. This is a space where power is exercised without reserve and where it becomes a sort of 'bare power' freely intervening on bare life.

Also, the Nazi regime demonstrates the generalisation of the state of emergency to the point where it becomes a permanent state. In the Nazi state the legal form of the state itself became the suspension of the rule of law. This made anything possible as the 'law', which existed only in its suspension. It is also created the situation whereby the camps achieved a new permanence as the materialisation of this 'state of exception'. As Agamben writes '*The camp is the space opened when the state of exception begins to become the rule*' (HS: 168–9). When the state of emergency or exception becomes the rule then we can have the camps as spaces of this indistinct state. What the camps do is contain this zone of indistinction, and inside the space of the camps there is an indistinction between exception and rule, fact and law, rule and application. This does not mean that power loses its purchase, but instead power operates in this space by incessantly deciding on these unstable oppositions. If this problem of the state of emergency did not end with Nazism, but has even become worse, then the camps remain a permanent possibility.

Another example is the regime of Alfredo Stroessner (b. 1912), President and dictator of Paraguay from 1954 to 1989, 'which brought the logic of the state of exception to its unsurpassed absurd extreme' (Zizek, 2002: 106). His regime was characterised by human rights abuses and the systematic use of torture, as well as turning Paraguay into a haven for Nazi war criminals. It also operated by the suspension of the rule of law and the institution of a permanent state of emergency. This state would only be rescinded for elections, although Stroessner was sometimes the only candidate standing. The elections would then 'legitimise' his rule, sometimes returning him to rule with a 90 per cent majority. As Slavoj Zizek has noted, 'The paradox is that the state of emergency was the normal state, while "normal" democratic freedom was the briefly enacted exception. Did not this weird regime merely spell out in advance the most radical consequence of a tendency that is clearly perceptible in our liberal-democratic societies in the aftermath of September 11?' (2002: 107). The rhetoric of the 'war against terrorism' is permitting the potential suspension of the rule of law, and the creation of new camps, such as Camp Delta in Guantánamo Bay, Cuba (which I shall discuss in Chapter Six).

Although Agamben's arguments may explain certain forms of camp, give new insights into the legal and political structures that are incarnated there and help illuminate our current situation, they are profoundly inadequate as an explanation of the Holocaust. Agamben does not consider the distinction between the concentration camps and the extermination camps, nor does he consider the vast literature on the implementation of the 'final solution'.[2] Instead, despite his protestations, he risks collapsing what was specific about this experience into a general account of 'the camps'. How can we talk of the exposure of bare life when, in the extermination or death camps, the killing process was like a 'conveyor belt' (Hilberg, 1985: 243)? If we are to consider modern death through the concept of exposure then it is necessary to be precise about exactly how this exposure operated in particular circumstances. This is a severe weakness of Agamben's work, particularly in relation to the Holocaust. As we shall see, his attempts to be more precise about what sort of exposure of bare life to death happened in the Holocaust are highly controversial and questionable. Despite the fact that Foucault did not make a direct comment on the camps some of his comments about Nazism actually make clear the failings of Agamben's work.

FOUCAULT AND AGAMBEN ON NAZISM

In Volume I of *The History of Sexuality* and in his lectures at the Collège de France, *'Society Must be Defended'*, Foucault took up the case of Nazism. What Nazism demonstrates, he argued, was the possibility of combining sovereign power, as the power to make die, with biopower, as the power to make live. He considers it to be 'the most cunning and the most naïve (and the former because of the latter) combination of the fantasies of blood and the paroxysms of disciplinary power' (Foucault, 1979a: 149). In combining sovereignty and biopower Nazism condensed the ability to make die, associated with the old power of death, with the ability to make live, associated with the new disciplinary powers over life. How did it blend these two forms of power together? It did so through 'fantasies of blood', which return to the past, but, through biopower, these fantasies were exercised across whole populations. What Nazi society had done was to have generalised biopower and also generalised the sovereign right to make die.

The integration of fantasies of blood with biopower is made possible by racism. Racism introduces the power of death into biopolitics by performing two functions: first, it permits the introduction of a break into the biological continuum of life, 'between what must live and what must die' (Foucault, 2003: 254). Therefore power is not simply biopower that takes all life as its object. With biopower life is the object of power up to the limit of death, when individuals or populations are then 'allowed' to die: let die. What racism permits is a division between the operations of biopower across populations, but then also a break that allows the operation of sovereign power to 'make die'. Second, racism makes the mass killing possible through the claim of biological purity, the 'fantasies of blood' that Foucault had spoken of. However, for Foucault, it is only in Nazi society (and certain socialist states) that we witness this deadly combination of sovereignty and biopower through racism.

The question that Foucault poses to Agamben is that of racism. Agamben's account of the camps as the result of the dislocating effects of the prevalence of bare life has no particular place for dealing with Nazism as an ideology or world-view of racism, which values some forms of life and leaves others to be exterminated. However, Agamben argues that racism is not the prime motivation of the Nazi camps. This is a highly counter-intuitive argument and highly dubious as well. According to the historian Mark Roseman, in his account of the path of Nazi thinking that led to the Holocaust, 'recent research has begun to rediscover the power of anti-Semitism as a guiding principle, less for the German population as a whole than for an important and influential minority within German society' (2002: 15). It appears that Nazi racial and anti-Semitic ideology is necessary to understand the Holocaust. Why then does Agamben not consider it a primary factor?

In his recent work *Remnants of Auschwitz* (1999) Agamben rejects Foucault's idea that racism is what divides up individuals and populations under Nazism. Although he recognises that racism is the explicit ideology of Nazism, he suggests that the Nazi division of life into life to be preserved and life 'unworthy of life' is actually the result of trying to produce and isolate bare life. The camps are not factories for the production of death but they are factories for the production of bare life reduced to an 'absolute biopolitical substance' (RA: 85). There is some similarity between this argument about the Holocaust and the work of the sociologist Zygmunt Bauman. His book *Modernity and the Holocaust* (1991) sees the Holocaust as rooted in aspects of the modern mentality and modern social organisation rather than in racism *per se*. In particular he focuses on the effects of rationalisation and bureaucratic planning as central factors, so the Holocaust is not an aberration of modern culture but made possible by it. As he states, 'It was the combination of growing potency of means and the unconstrained determination to use it in the service of an artificial, designed order, that gave human cruelty its distinctive *modern* touch and made the Gulag, Auschwitz and Hiroshima possible' (Bauman, 1991: 219).

Where Bauman argues for the importance of rational planning and social engineering, Agamben argues for the importance of the separation of bare life. Neither account necessarily involves excluding racism as a factor. Bauman certainly does not and racism also plays a part in Agamben's account of the separation of bare life. However, both accounts tend to stress how the Holocaust involves other, more general, features of modern culture. In Agamben's case what we find in the camps is a form of sovereign power that is not concerned with making us die, or making us live, but with making us survive. How can Agamben ignore the massive role of racism in Nazism? What justifies his claim that power is about enforced survival when we consider Nazism as a work of extermination? His answer to these questions is that sovereign power in the Nazi camps is not simply organised around death and extermination but organised around the production of an extreme form of bare life.

This extreme form of bare life, which is perhaps the most extreme form of bare life, is the *Muselmann* or 'Muslim'. The 'Muslim' was the camp jargon for the inmate reduced to a state of living death, and the term seems to come from the European and Western fantasy of fatalism imputed to Muslims. One survivor of the camps described a 'Muslim' as 'a staggering corpse, a bundle of physical functions in its last convulsions' (in RA: 41). This term also depends on 'race', in the wider sense of European racism towards the Muslim world. Although Agamben deals with the various differences in terminology used to describe inmates reduced to this state, he does not consider how racism could also play a part in this reduction to the extreme limit of being bare life. Particularly he does not consider this strange and terrible intersection between anti-Semitism and Western racism more generally around the figure of the 'Muslims'.

They were, as the Auschwitz survivor Primo Levi said, 'the drowned' and formed 'the backbone of the camp, an anonymous mass' (in RA: 44). Agamben takes this concept and extends it to the point where he argues that the Nazi camps were 'also, and above all, the site of the production of the *Muselmann*, the final biopolitical substance to be isolated in the biological continuum. Beyond the *Muselmann* lies only the gas chamber' (RA: 85). But can we really say that the camps are 'above all' the sites of the production of bare life? Certainly we need to understand more the terrible experience of the 'Muslim', and Agamben is right to draw attention to this element of the Holocaust. The 'Muslim' demonstrates an extreme form of exposure to death that is without precedent, due to the deliberate reduction of human beings into this state of 'living death'. As many commentators have noted Agamben draws our attention to this phenomenon in a startling and disturbing fashion – especially by drawing out of this situation new concepts of ethics and politics.

However, his remarks remain suggestive rather than being firmly based in the historical evidence. While the 'Muslim' may be the 'faceless centre' of the concentration camps, is the really true of the extermination camps? Agamben's confusion of these two forms of camp means that he does not properly confront the camps as factories of death and not of bare life. Again his choice to focus on Auschwitz, which combined the functions of concentration camp and extermination camp, is what allows him to evade this problem. It also allows him to minimise the question of racism and genocide. Although Nazism functions through racism, Agamben argues that in the 'Muslim' we find the figure of the almost absolute separation of bare life from political life or national or ethnic identity, and the production by power of 'a bare, unassignable and unwitnessable life' (RA: 157). While Nazism begins from the ideology of 'racial' identity, in the camps we find a form of life that lacks any sort of identity at all, except as bare life. This form of bare life is not living but not yet dead; instead it is bare life reduced by power to the state of survival. It incarnates bare life that is deprived of all identity and totally saturated by power. Being between life and death the 'Muslim' exists in 'the non-place in which all disciplinary barriers are destroyed and all embankments flooded' (RA: 48). This means that the camps, as a space of power, have ruined the concept of life by producing bare life that threatens to undo power at the same time as it is absolutely exposed to power. Although the camp was supposed to localise the zone of indistinction in which power operates, that localisation finds its limit in the 'Muslim'.

What Foucault insists on, and which is necessary, is a more thorough consideration of how the biological continuum of existence is divided through racism. It is this division that then seems to make possible the further 'production' of bare life. Also, we can be rightly sceptical that the 'aim' of the camps was to produce bare life. Agamben's own insistence that power is thanatopolitical, and that bare life is always life exposed to death, needs to be retained alongside his remarks about sovereign power producing bare life as survival. He may alert us to new ways in which we are exposed to death but he is in danger of minimising the actual process of extermination. While Agamben's use of the term 'camps' leads to imprecision in his work, his arguments concerning our exposure to death can be given a more precise sense if his work is developed further. Instead of setting up a simplistic continuity between the Nazi camps and other 'camps' (the Soviet gulags, the camps of the war in the former Yugoslavia, Camp Delta, etc.) we could use his analysis of thanatopolitics and sovereign power as the power to enforce survival to produce a more detailed reading of how we are exposed to death in these places.

Agamben is right to note the absence of any consideration of the camps in Foucault's analysis of spaces of power. The emergence of new forms of camp in the conflict in the former Yugoslavia and in the 'war against terrorism', to give just two examples, suggests the necessity of analysing what legal and political structures of power are at work in these spaces. It seems that in these spaces power takes on the form of 'bare power', operating with impunity on the bodies of the inmates. Agamben's prophecy that 'we must expect not only new camps but also always new and more lunatic regulative definitions of the inscription of life in the city' (HS: 176) is being fulfilled. It is not only a matter of new camps but of new spaces that take on similar forms to the camps; these might include detention centres, security cordons and suspects being held in prisons or police stations under conditions that leave them vulnerable to sovereign power. Therefore, his warnings concerning the persistence of the camps as a possibility of power in modern culture, and how this possibility does not exist only in what we would name as 'camps', need to be addressed if we are to analyse our exposure to death.

What is also crucial is his insistence that our exposure to death be thought of as an exposure to power. This exposure requires us to closely analyse the space in which this power is exercised and the nature of power. Of course this will vary historically, and so any analysis of the culture of death will have to address changes in the culture of power as well. Agamben's arguments concerning sovereign power as the form of power in the West and its operation through the ban offer us powerful models for engaging with these problems. His suggestion that power today has entered a 'zone of indistinction' allows us to understand the fragmentation of modern power without conceding that power lacks a space or that it finds its limits in death. This work has gained relevance due to the new political and legal situations that have been introduced in Western democracies following the September 11 attacks. Finally, his suggestion that power can operate through forcing us to survive in a state between life and death is important in offering us new ways to understand how power exposes us to death.

CONCLUSION: MODERN DEATH OR POSTMODERN DEATH?

What are the implications of these arguments concerning death and power for our understanding of the culture of death, especially modern death? Cultural studies academics have often promoted new models of power that emphasise its fluidity, dispersion and fragmentation. This fragmentation of power is then seen as an opportunity that opens a space for new flexible identities that would slip between the gaps. The celebration of the politics of lifestyles could even be extended to the politics of 'deathstyles' as well. Death would be just another product in the postmodern cultural supermarket, and we could choose our style of death from any number of historically and culturally different forms. As the fragmentation of power fragments styles of life then it would also fragment styles of death. We could then slip between the gaps of power by constructing our own personal 'deathstyle', our own postmodern version of the 'good death', if, of course, we have the economic and cultural power to do so. This would be a new 'postmodern' death.

Such a 'postmodern' celebration of the fragmentation of power is problematic if we consider the fragmentation of power as the spread of power across culture. Instead of new gaps opening up in power, where we could craft new identities, these gaps and spaces may simply open new effects of power. The spectre of sovereign power has not disappeared but appears everywhere. This suggests the importance of the analysis of power to our analysis of the culture of death. What we have found is that the new extent of our exposure to death is the result of the extent of our exposure to power in the 'zone of indistinction'. This model also suggests that we are not in a situation where we would have a postmodern choice over either our lifestyle or our 'deathstyle'. As we have seen the space of power operates by separating off bare life and imposing on us legal and political identities. Any celebration of the choice of identity, or of death, that does not recognise the problem of bare life can only end up condoning the spread of power rather than challenging it. To claim the power to choose our own death is only to disguise the operations of power that still takes death as its object.

If we cannot celebrate these effects of fragmentation then we also cannot celebrate the value of survival. Of course, this does not mean that survival is of no value at all, but Agamben alerts us to the fact that in modern culture survival can be another form of our exposure to death. The nightmare of life reduced to pure survival did not begin or end with the destruction of Nazism, and is present today in new spaces of power. This reduction of bare life to pure survival is also not confined to the third world but, as a result of new developments in medical technology, we face power that can produce 'the nightmare of a vegetative life that indefinitely survives the life or relation, a non-human life infinitely separable from human existence' (RA: 154). The absolute separation of bare life that we find in the figure of the 'Muslim' can also be found in 'the body of the overcomatose person and the neomort attached to life-support systems today' (RA: 156). I now want to move into this new space of power to analyse how death has become thoroughly politicised in modern culture.

NOTES

1. The 'zone of indistinction' is obviously difficult to define because it concerns the state of indistinction and exception. Briefly, it refers to how the spreading of bare life and the spreading of sovereign power in modern culture make it difficult to define or grasp the place of power.

2. The classic account remains Raul Hilberg's *The Destruction of the European Jews* (1985), and see also the web sites listed in the bibliography. For a useful introduction to the historiography of the Holocaust see R. J. B. Bosworth's book *Explaining Auschwitz and Hiroshima* (1994).

CHAPTER 3

Politicising Death

INTRODUCTION: THE HOSPITAL ROOM

One of the major spaces of death in modern culture is the hospital room, where we face death alone surrounded by medical technology. The surrealist film-maker Luis Buñuel (1900–1983) reflected on this in his autobiography, *My Last Breath* (1985). Buñuel is the celebrated director of avant-garde films, including *Un Chien Andalou* (1928), made in collaboration with the artist Salvador Dali. That film contains one of the most shocking images in the history of film, of a razor being drawn across the eye of a young woman. His autobiography ends with him pondering his own death and he writes that the worst death 'is one that's kept at bay by the miracles of modern medicine, a death that never ends. In the name of Hippocrates, doctors have invented the most exquisite form of torture ever known to man: survival. Sometimes I even pitied Franco, kept alive artificially for months at the cost of incredible suffering' (1985: 256). In 1975 General Franco, the then Spanish head of state, suffered several heart attacks and then a number of other medical complications and surgical interventions. What led Buñuel to pity Franco was that 'Thereafter, he was kept alive by a massive panoply of life-support machines, regaining consciousness occasionally to murmur "how hard it is to die"' (Preston, 1995: 778). In the name of survival, even if that survival is at the cost of intense suffering, medical science forced Franco into the position of bare life sustained without even the 'release' of death.

In his lecture course of 1976 Michel Foucault also commented on the death of Franco. He regarded it as an example of the shift away from sovereign power and towards the rise of biopower. As he said, Franco 'fell under the influence of a power that managed life so well, that took so little heed of death, … he didn't even realize that he was dead and was being kept alive after his death' (Foucault, 2003: 248–9). The sovereign's power to inflict bloody death has passed over into a biopolitical management of life that no longer has any real awareness of death at all, and where even the sovereign is subject to biopolitics. This biopolitics tries so hard to preserve life, even at the cost of terrible suffering, because death is the limit to its power.[1] Agamben sees this scene very differently. Death is not the limit of biopower but is what is politicised by biopower. We have not left sovereignty behind but Franco, a traditional sovereign, is subject to sovereignty in a new form: the power of doctors to decide on life, death and survival.

The scene in Franco's hospital room demonstrates that sovereign power is no longer political in the traditional sense, the matter of the head of state or government. Instead, it has entered into the zone of indistinction where this power over life and death also becomes the domain of the doctor. The space of power is still the space of sovereignty but now the space of sovereignty can be occupied by new figures that take up the 'old power of death'. In this chapter the process of the dispersion of sovereign power into the zone of indistinction will be examined. First, this requires us to venture into the hospital room as one of the zones where sovereign power is taken up by new figures: not only the doctor, but also priests, philosophers, lawyers, patients and their families and advocates. In particular, we must focus on the situation when patients are sustained by life-support machines in a state of survival that transforms them into an almost pure version of bare life. In this situation we shall see how the decision on the time of death takes place in a particular space of power, thereby bringing together my arguments from the first two chapters.

Although the sovereign, as head of state, is no longer dominant, this does not mean that death is no longer political. Rather, this political power has become indistinct and dispersed, but it still exists in the decision on the time of death. This does not mean that death is becoming less political; rather it means that death is becoming more and more politicised. This is because the political power over death is penetrating further into our bodies, as it can either sustain or end life in more extreme circumstances. It is another instance of a new form of our exposure to death in modern culture, as medical technology allows survival to the point where to talk of 'life' hardly seems to make sense any more. What we must do is look behind the masks of power that today conceal the persistence of sovereign power. This means that we must not simply accept the argument that modern death is medical death. Although death in the West often takes place in the hospital room, or through the authorisation of medicine, when the doctor signs the death certificate, for example, death is still political. Despite the fact that advances in medical technology are significant for our culture of death, death is not solely a technical matter.

Instead, what stands behind the medical decision on death is the old power of death associated with sovereign power. This old power has taken on new masks in modern culture but it has not disappeared. To strip away these masks is not to indulge in nostalgia for the time where sovereign power did not disguise its brutality. Instead, it is to expose the thorough politicisation of death that persists despite the power of death no longer appearing as 'strictly' political. The theatre of power is no longer the scene of execution where, as Foucault described, the body of the sovereign confronts the body of the accused in a staging of death. If modern power has entered the zone of indistinction then the theatre of power has become spread across our culture, including into medicine. The phrase 'operating theatre' suggests this staged element of medical practice. These are no longer the relatively 'open' spaces they used to be, but they are still highly staged rituals.

The artist Orlan explores this through her 'performances' in which she undergoes plastic surgery. These are carefully staged, with costumes from famous designers and readings of relevant texts, and they are also broadcast or recorded (see Ince, 2000). Another example of the exploration of the theatre of medical power is David Cronenberg's film *Dead Ringers* (1988). Again the operations carried out in this film become rituals, with surgical gowns transformed into bizarre costumes and medical instruments becoming strange sculptures. These artists are exploring the world of medical power, but they remain at the level of questioning medical power. Also, although they reveal the theatrical elements of this power, they do not go far enough in revealing our exposure to death. They turn what is supposedly 'private' into a public spectacle, but, if we examine the hospital room as a space of power, then we can see that it blurs the distinction between public and private. This is the result of the hidden political dimension of our exposure to death by medical power.

DEATH IN MOTION

In 1959 two French neurophysiologists, P. Mollaret and M. Goulon, identified a new and extreme form of coma, which they called coma *dépassé* ('overcoma'). It was extreme because in this new form of coma 'the total abolition of relational life functions corresponds to an equally total abolition of vegetative life functions' (Mollaret and Goulon in HS: 160). What this means is that there is barely any existence of life at all in this state; not only does the coma victim have no means to communicate but also their bodily functions have to be sustained if they are to survive. The result is a strange new form of life existing on the verge of death. This new form of life was made possible by advances in medical technology with the invention of life-support machines. These technologies, through artificially sustaining breathing and heart function, create a stage of life that appears to be hardly recognisable as life. In fact, we could ask what sort of survival is this, what sort of life is this, if it is a 'life' at all?

It is these questions that have led to the development of a new way of determining death. The traditional criteria of death were the stopping of the heartbeat and the cessation of breathing, but, because of the life-support machines, the overcomatose patient's heart still beats and they still breathe. By these criteria they are still alive, but because they seem to exist in a state of virtual death, as death in motion, then new criteria of death had to be developed. This problem was made more pressing because, in a strange coincidence, the development of life-support technologies was accompanied by the development of new transplant technologies. The body of the overcomatose patient is ideal for the needs of transplantation, as the organs are kept undamaged and alive. However, to permit transplantation, that is, the removal of organs from the overcomatose patient for use, new legal criteria of death are required. Without these criteria the surgeon performing the organ removal would be liable to the charge of murder.

Therefore, in 1968, a special Harvard University medical school committee developed the new concept of 'brain death'. This committee consisted of ten members of the medical profession, a lawyer, a historian and a theologian. The selection of the committee is an interesting example of how the decision on death might be moving into the zone of indistinction. As we can see, the medical profession is dominant, but there is also a representative of the law, of academic knowledge and of theology. The sovereign decision on death is being taken up by new fields of expertise, and has been displaced from the head of state. What is striking about the committee's final report is that it was so open about the reasons for the new definition of death. The beginning of the report indicates two reasons for the new definition: the first is 'the burden' patients in an irreversible coma place on themselves and on the health care system, although it is not clear how this could be a burden on the patient; the second reason is that the old criteria for death have led to problems in obtaining organs for transplantation. In fact, an earlier draft of the report had been even more explicit about this second reason: 'An issue of secondary but by no means minor importance is that with increased experience and knowledge and development in transplantation there is great need for tissues and organs of, among others, the patient whose cerebrum has been hopelessly destroyed, in order to restore those who are salvageable' (in Singer, 1994: 25).

It is clear that the change in the definition of death was driven by the needs of transplantation and not by conceptual problems with the previous definition of death. What then is 'brain death'? It is the irreversible loss of all the functions of the brain, which is defined by the lack of electrical activity, measured by an EEG, the lack of blood flow to the brain, determined by blood flow studies, and the absence of brain function, assessed by clinical tests. Although this new definition was intended to clarify the concept of death, instead it introduces a wavering into the time of death. The first evidence of this wavering is that the new criteria of brain death do not simply replace the traditional criteria of death (cessation of heart function and breathing). Instead brain death is defined as the fact that if life-support technology were withdrawn then the patient would then die, in the traditional sense. As Agamben notes, the partisans of brain death do not hesitate to appeal to the idea that brain death leads to death, when, of course, by the new criteria the patient must and should already be dead. There is then a wavering in the very definition of death, which the concept of brain death does not resolve but holds within itself.

The philosopher Peter Singer, whose work I shall discuss in detail in Chapter Four, has also pointed out this conceptual confusion. It means that it remains difficult to think of the brain-dead as dead, and even doctors and nurses who work with the 'brain-dead' often refer to the patient as still alive. So, when asked what they would say to the family of a patient determined to be brain-dead, replies included: 'The machine is basically what's keeping him alive' (in Singer, 1994: 34). By the criteria of brain death the patient is, precisely, not alive but to the medical professional familiar with the criteria the patient is alive. Singer suggests two reasons for this persistent inability to think of the brain-dead as dead, either we remain attached to obsolete definitions of death, or the patients are not really dead. It might be a matter of psychological adjustment to this new state of affairs but if we examine the situation in Agamben's terms we can see that it is not so much a question of adjusting to a new definition of death. Instead the new definition of death is itself viciously circular, and our inability to adjust to it is a reflection of the conceptual ambiguity encoded within the concept of brain death.

This first wavering over the definition of death is accompanied by second wavering over the authority to decide on the time of death: does this belong to medicine or law? Is the judgement that a patient is brain-dead a legal or a medical decision? Agamben describes the 1974 case where a defence lawyer for Andrew D. Lyons argued that his client had not committed murder by gunshot but that the surgeon, Norman Shumway, had caused the death of the victim by removing his heart for transplantation. This defence, although ingenious, was not successful and the doctor was not charged. However, the grounds on which Dr Shumway declared his innocence are problematic: 'I'm saying anyone whose brain is dead is dead. It is the one determinant that would be universally applicable, because the brain is the one organ that can't be transplanted' (in HS: 163). This can hardly be a solution as the logic of the doctor's argument means that if we were to evolve a new technology that allowed brain transplantation then brain death would no longer be death. It has simply shifted the problem, rather than resolving it. Also, this case demonstrates the conflict between medical and legal power in defining death; is death a matter to be decided on by doctors or by the courts?

Despite these problems, brain death has gained widespread, and rapid, acceptance as the new criterion of death. Singer writes of a 'revolution without opposition' (1994: 28), although he also suggests that brain death is, at best, only a 'convenient fiction' or 'unstable compromise' (1994: 35). Of course, we might wonder if even the 'traditional' criteria of death that Agamben invokes are secure. There have been, and still are, widespread fears of being buried alive. In Chapter One I mentioned Edgar Allan Poe's short story 'The Premature Burial', which plays on these fears. It may well be, then, that we have not passed from a stable traditional definition of death to an unstable modern definition of death, but rather from one form of wavering around the time of death to another. The time of death has always been problematic but this problem takes on a new and more stark form: 'And today, in discussions of *ex lege* definitions of new criteria for death, it is a further identification of this bare life – which is now severed from all cerebral activity and subjects – that still decides if a particular body will be considered alive or, instead, abandoned to the extreme vicissitudes of transplantation' (P: 232).

What Agamben insists on is that the debate around the definition of death in modern culture is one that rests on the unspoken biopolitical ground of 'a further identification of this bare life'. It may be that we are better able to account for the rapid acceptance of brain death, despite its conceptual problems, because of its compatibility with Western biopolitics rather than, simply, because of its convenience. If the decision on the time of death is a decision on the identification of bare life, then this decision must be political and not 'natural'. The problem is that some of Agamben's formulations around the traditional criteria of death suggest that once death was natural, or at least simpler, and that now it is political. Instead, if Western politics has always been biopolitics, then death has always been political and can only be in the process of becoming further or more extensively politicised. Agamben's ambiguity on this point suggests that the wavering around the time of death has infected his own work.

This is particularly clear if we turn to literature. The two great Western tragedies Sophocles' *Antigone* and Shakespeare's *Hamlet* both raise the question of the time of death. They do so by considering the rites that might be required to declare the dead dead, and the political nature of this decision. In particular, they both focus on the role of sovereign power in this decision.

In the case of *Antigone* the tragedy is the result of the decision by Creon, the King of Thebes, not to allow proper burial for Polyneices, brother of Antigone. His decision to leave Polyneices' body exposed to nature and Antigone's decision to bury his body despite this edict are what set this tragedy in motion. With *Hamlet*, the crisis in Denmark is caused by the problem of the King's murder and then his 'appearance' as a ghost. Again, this refusal of a proper death leads to the tragedy of Hamlet's famously delayed revenge. However, these two plays are not only about the time of death, they are also about the time of mourning and what a 'proper' mourning might be. We might consider the ongoing crisis in the time of death as an ongoing crisis of mourning as well – perhaps even that mourning itself is an experience of crisis that lacks a certain closure.[2]

The importance of Agamben's work is that it demonstrates that the issues of brain death and the bare life of the overcomatose patient cannot be considered outside the context of biopolitics. These issues, and the wavering we find there, are the result of the time of death entering the zone of indistinction that characterises modern culture. The two incidents of wavering affect when someone is dead and who decides when someone is dead. Who, then, decides on the time of death in modern culture? In examining the case of the overcomatose patient we have seen the conflict between the right of medicine to decide the time of death and the right of the law. For Agamben, the perfect example of this wavering is the case of Karen Ann Quinlan. A summary of this important case has been provided by Helga Kuhse and Peter Singer, which indicates how the decision on the time of death is at stake:

> It was not until 1976 that a landmark US case – that of Karen Ann Quinlan – lent support to the view that doctors had no legal duty to prolong life in all circumstances. Karen Ann Quinlan, who had become comatose in 1975, was attached to a respirator to assist her breathing. Her condition was described as 'chronic persistent vegetative state'. When the treating doctor refused to honour the family's wishes that Karen be removed from the respirator, the case eventually came before the New Jersey Supreme Court, which decided that life-support could be discontinued without the treating doctor being deemed to have committed an act of unlawful homicide. (Kuhse and Singer, 1998: 9)

What happened next was that, although life-support was withdrawn, Karen Ann Quinlan began to breathe naturally and survived, through artificial nutrition, until 1985, the year of her natural 'death'. As we can see from this description, power over life and death passes from the family's wishes to the legal profession and then back to the medical profession.

It should be noted that Karen Ann Quinlan was not 'brain-dead', at least by the criteria of whole brain death, which accounts for the need for a legal decision on this case. If the doctors had withdrawn life-support without this permission they would have been guilty of murder. Agamben is fascinated not only by the legal and medical issues around this case but more by the strange state into which she passed after life-support was withdrawn: 'It is clear that Karen Quinlan's body had, in fact, entered a zone of indetermination in which the words "life" and "death" had lost their meaning, and which, at least in this sense, is not unlike the space of exception inhabited by bare life' (HS: 164). Why does her body inhabit the space of bare life? In being sustained by medical technology Karen Ann Quinlan has been subject to a separation of her bare biological life from her political and legal identity. She becomes an example of an almost pure form of bare life.

One issue that Agamben does not discuss is the fact that the body that is exposed to death is the body of a woman. It seems that he shares the widespread assumption that sexual difference does not matter in the face of death. Those feminist theorists who work within death studies have insisted, on the contrary, that we recognise that '*death is gendered*' (Goodwin and Bronfen, 1993: 20). To ignore this fact is to ignore the fact that our exposure to death is also often constructed through gender. The dead female body, or the female body exposed to death, has often been an object of aesthetic fascination. The American writer Edgar Allan Poe notoriously remarked, in his essay 'The Philosophy of Composition' (1846), 'the death, then, of a beautiful woman is, unquestionably, the most poetic topic in the world' (1999: 4). Elisabeth Bronfen has called her history of death, femininity and the aesthetic *Over Her Dead Body* (1992). Agamben does not address the fact that, in this case, bare life is found 'over her dead body'.

Despite the fact that Karen Quinlan's body is 'reduced' to its biological minimum, it is, at the same time, absolutely subject to the legal decision on the time of death. This legal decision acts upon, and totally imprints, the body as bare life or biological remnant. Therefore she is not withdrawn from power into the biological but exposed all the more to the sovereign decision on death through being abandoned to the state of death in motion. The result is that the decision on death is not simply medical or legal but, in fact, political. Agamben insists that the decision on life and death is not a scientific or a medical matter, and we have seen the problems that science and medicine have with defining death. Rather, death acquires a political meaning through the act of sovereign decision that decides on death. It is the wavering state of the overcomatose patient that calls for a decision, and this decision takes place in the space of power of sovereignty.

This decision is made particularly urgent because of the state to which the overcomatose patient is reduced as a result of medical technology. They have become 'a purely bare life' (HS: 164), or the 'extreme embodiment of *homo sacer*' (HS: 165). What we can see, in the hospital room, is the reappearance of the sacred man, or woman, who may be killed and yet not sacrificed. Also, the hospital room exists as the zone of indistinction, where it is the indistinct status of this body, wavering between life and death and wavering between medicine and law, which constantly calls for the sovereign decision. What this makes clear is that power is not, as Foucault claimed, rendered impotent before death. Power does not find its limit in death, but, instead, this wavering at the point of death is what permits our exposure to death without any limit. In a way, power escapes any idea of death as its limit through enforced survival, which allows it to extend into the body and to saturate the body with power. This depth of exposure to death may be one of the signs of modern death and of the extent of our exposure to death in modern culture.

THE LIVING DEAD

This is even more evident if we consider the possibility, mentioned by Agamben, of the emergence of 'neomorts' (HS: 164). These 'neomorts' would have the legal status of corpses but be kept 'alive', in a state of coma, so that their organs would be available for transplantation. This anxiety is given its most paranoid and disturbing form in Michael Crichton's 1977 film *Coma*. In that film a doctor (played by the actress Genevieve Bujold) uncovers a conspiracy where patients are deliberately put into coma and then 'stored' so their organs can be 'harvested' for transplantation. These 'neomorts' are, literally, kept in a state of suspension as they are hung from wires in a large storage facility. The body of the coma victim is reduced to 'meat' by being hung like an animal carcass in a slaughterhouse. Bare life is here, as Agamben says, 'defined as an intermediary being between man and animal' (HS: 165). This is the vision of an absolute politicisation of bare life, in which the body is completely subject to the vicissitudes of medical science, whether that be transplantation or experimentation. The anxiety expressed here is more extreme than we find in films that play on the horror of our own and others' bodies, such as the so-called 'body horror' films of David Cronenberg, John Carpenter, George A. Romero and others.

For example, in the fashion for zombie films during the 1970s and 1980s (particularly in Italy and the United States) we find bare life, life between life and death as, literally, 'death in motion'. However, despite the horror of these 'creatures', they still possess agency, even if that is only the pursuit and destruction of human beings. These films may often be intentionally (as in Dan O'Bannon's 1984 film *Return of the Living Dead*) or unintentionally amusing, but they still fix on a particular modern anxiety: that of life reduced to bare life as an absolute horror. The recent British film *28 Days Later* (Danny Boyle, UK, 2002) updates these anxieties for the new millennium. It concerns the spread to humans of a rage-inducing virus as the result of antivivisectionists freeing infected monkeys, producing the 'infecteds'. The film plays on fears of cross-species disease (after AIDS), and fears of medical experimentation leading to catastrophe. Despite the fact that the director insists that the 'infecteds' are not 'zombies', they obey the form of the zombie film, except that they display a kinetic violence not usually associated with the traditional 'shuffling' zombie. In fact, the current remake of *Dawn of the Dead* (2004) also takes up this new rapid-moving zombie. In *28 Days Later* the threat is one of violent agency and urban breakdown (the initial scenes are set in London), perhaps even of feral animality. Here bare life as the indistinction of life and death is crossed with bare life as the indistinction of human and animal.

These films may actually guard us against another fear. This is the fear explored in *Coma*, where we face our possible reduction to absolute bare life with no agency left whatsoever. The body of bare life suspended in the state of exception is simply held awaiting its use, and left vulnerable to whatever decision might be made upon it. The 'neomorts' are denied any agency at all and medicine can pursue its experimentation without limits. This absolute politicisation of bare life is also visible in the demands by certain scientists for a kind of nationalisation of the body by the state. The reasons given are to make organs available for transplantation and bodies available for experimentation, but the consequences are an extension of sovereign power. It appears that our bodies are under threat of becoming, virtually, possessions of the state. This nationalisation of the body threatens to extend further even than some of the proposals entertained by Nazi biopoliticians. Also, it helps substantiate Agamben's claims for the continuities between totalitarian states and democracies. At the thanatopolitical level, there are frightening similarities, which are being carried further by the politicisation of bare life: what is being extended and dispersed is the capacity to make decisions on life and death.

Although medical technology is crucial to this process, these new forms of clinical 'death' are not simply the result of technological advances. Rather than being the victory of the technologicisation of death, what we are witnessing is the absolute politicisation of death through the capacities of technology to further identify and decide on bare life. Therefore, the historian Philippe Ariès is incorrect when he argues 'Death is a technical phenomenon obtained by a cessation of care, a cessation determined in a more or less avowed way by a decision of the doctor and the hospital team' (1974: 88). The decision is what is still crucial, and this decision is not technical nor, as we shall see in the next chapter, is it ethical, but it is political. How is this power exercised?

THE MASKS OF POWER

The decision on the line to be drawn between life and death is, for Agamben, fundamentally political. It is only the political decision of sovereign power that can decide on the wavering of bare life caught in, to use Agamben's expression, the 'no-man's land' between life and death. What is wavering is not only the decision on the time of death but also who has the power to make that decision. The death of Franco demonstrated that the sovereign is no longer the singular figure of power over life and death (if that were ever simply the case, of course) but also subject to that power. Agamben had already made clear that sovereign power is not so much the possession of an individual but a decision that articulates the relation of politics and life. Today, that articulation of politics and life passes outside the recognised figure of the sovereign and into other figures: the doctor, the priest, the lawyer, the philosopher and the patients, their advocates and relatives. The blurring of the line between life and death is what leads to these new figures acquiring the 'old power of death'.

What happens is that 'It is the invisible sovereign that stares at us behind the dull-witted masks of the powerful who, whether or not they realize it, govern us in its name' (ME: 8). The decision on death is carried out in the space of sovereign power, but this space has become so indistinct that it can include sites like the hospital room. Sovereign power has taken on new, and multiple, masks. These masks conceal it, making it invisible, but also make it proliferate, meaning that we confront the power over life and death at every turn. Today, this task is, increasingly, being carried out by medicine. This is what is often called the 'medicalisation of death'. However, if we follow Agamben's analysis of our exposure to death we must be sceptical. It is not so much that death becomes medicalised, as that medicine takes up the old power of death.

Agamben's discussion of the politicisation of death through the spreading of sovereign power into medicine is restricted to the situation after the Second World War. He is content, as we have seen, to draw controversial connections between contemporary biomedical practice and the practices of Nazi biopolitics. In doing so he does take account of the medical meanings applied to death but only within a recent time frame. If his problem is the 'medicalisation' of life and death, then he gives a restricted and limited analysis of that process. One striking absence from his discussion is a work of which he is no doubt well aware, Michel Foucault's *The Birth of the Clinic* (1963). This book offers a history of modern medicine as a space of power, which originates in a shift at the end of the eighteenth century and the beginning of the nineteenth century. Foucault is particularly concerned with the question of death and how 'from the integration of death into medical thought is born a medicine that is given as a science of the individual' (1989a: 197). A detailed analysis of this work suggests that any understanding of the relationship between medicine and power needs to be extended beyond the limits of Agamben's account.

MEDICINE, POWER, AND DEATH

The Birth of the Clinic concentrates on how this historical shift in medicine rests on 'the stable, visible, legible basis of death' (Foucault, 1989a: 196). The analysis that Foucault makes of the mutation in medicine around death is ignored in his own later work on biopolitics. This is despite the fact that the mutation in medicine and the mutation in power take place at the same time. Perhaps Foucault's later concentration on power as the power over life forces him to ignore his own earlier insights into the integration of death into medical discourse. It may be that the earlier work poses problems that his later work prefers to ignore or downplay. Not only does it raise the question of death but also Foucault suggests that medicine operates through the 'sovereign power of the empirical gaze' (1989a: xiii). This retention of the category of sovereignty runs against his later argument that sovereignty is eclipsed with the rise of biopolitics. Also, in *The Birth of the Clinic* Foucault argues that the integration of death is central to the birth of a science and philosophy of the individual; this challenges his later assertion that it is sexuality which plays this role.

So *The Birth of the Clinic* is a forgotten work for both Foucault and Agamben. However, this work is crucial for understanding the links between medicine and power. At the centre of the book is the mutation in medicine that alters the place of death in medical discourse. In the eighteenth century death was absolutely beyond medicine. Its ambiguity threatened the organisation of medical discourse, which tried to keep death at bay. What was required was a new medical discourse that could master death and this would be supplied by the rise of pathological anatomy. With the study of death located in the clinic, pathological anatomy could now distinguish between effects of disease, death and decomposition because the time between death and autopsy was reduced dramatically. The result was a far more precise analysis of death, which revealed that not all bodily systems suffered 'death' at the same time. In fact, it would be better to think of a chain of deaths that occurred in the organism, for example first the death of the heart, then the lungs and finally the brain.

This means that when Philippe Ariès claimed that it is only recently that 'Death has been dissected, cut to bits by a series of little steps, which finally makes it impossible to know which step was the real death' (1974: 88–9) he was wrong. Instead, it was at the turn of the eighteenth century that medicine began to dissect death into a series of components. This gradual dissection of death allowed doctors to detach death from disease as well. Death was no longer to be confused with disease or mistaken for one of its effects, but it gained its own fixed mechanisms. Now death becomes the point from which medicine can analyse both life and disease. This took place because medicine turned its gaze on 'the immobile space of the dissected body' (Foucault, 1989a: 144). What this body offered was a means to fix and locate death. The clinic, as a space of power, took in and structured the body, fixing it as an immobile space. Foucault associates this new fixing of death into the body with the work of the French anatomist Bichat (1771–1802).

Bichat is considered to be the father of modern histology and tissue pathology. He helped relativise the concept of death into a series of partial deaths and he famously redefined life as exposure to death, writing that 'Life is the totality of functions that resist the absence of life' (in Foucault, 1989a: 145). This meant that his work was a thinking of life that defined life through a thinking of death; it is death that gives us the truth of life and disease. The importance he gives to death was influential in the organisation of medical discourse on the new basis of death. His work made clear that death could be analysed, broken into segments and so mastered by medical discourse that was organised within the space of the clinic. Death is no longer a threat to be feared but a principle of medicine or, as Foucault poetically puts it, 'The living night is dissipated in the brightness of death' (1989a: 146).

Foucault does not concentrate on the question of power in this work, however. But his remarks concerning the sovereign power of the empirical gaze and his suggestion that this gaze requires that the patient 'has to be enveloped in a collective, homogenous space' (1989a: 196) suggest that the space of the clinic is also a space of power. Foucault also makes clear that this integration of death in medical discourse works by locating death in the body of the individual. In the conclusion to *The Birth of the Clinic* Foucault draws connections between this location of death in the body and our contemporary fascination with death. He argues that the fact that 'generally speaking, the experience of individuality in modern culture is bound up with that of death' (1989a: 197) is a result of medical discourse defining the individual through death. The modern culture of the individual is the result of the exposure of the individual to death, now enclosed within the individual's body. It is the positive discourse of medicine that decides that, for us, the experience of death as the problem of the individual is *the* cultural and philosophical problem.

This fascination with the individual experience of death runs throughout contemporary culture. Foucault mentions the example of lyric poetry, which we might think is very far from the discourse of medicine. However, he argues that poetry's obsession with individual death is the result of medicine forming 'the dark, but firm web of our experience' (Foucault, 1989a: 199). The same is also true of philosophy, another discourse that has little directly to do with medicine. The contemporary philosopher Simon Critchley, in his book *Very Little ... Almost Nothing* (1997), demonstrates that modern philosophy has been preoccupied with the problem of finitude, the problem that we will die. Foucault explains this as the result of medical discourse forcing us to define our individuality through death.

In his history of sexuality Foucault would abandon this idea that death defined our individuality. Instead, he would argue that sexuality would play that role, and this would fit with the idea that power is focused on life in modern culture. His earlier work is actually closer to the work of Agamben, and it seems to suggest that biopolitics, the politics of life, must be considered as thanatopolitics, the politics of death. Could we also not see the birth of the clinic as a result of the isolation of bare life? What the clinic depends on is the immobilised corpse and the ability to progressively define particular chains of death. Bare life, located within the clinical space, is subject to the sovereign power of medical discourse that slices into the body, analysing its exposure to death as it seizes upon it. Also, this discourse belongs to a dissemination of bare life into the body of the subject as individual. What makes us individuals is our exposure to death, and this is created by medical discourse that decides upon the time of death in a space of power. This time is, already, dispersed into various *times* of death: of the heart, the lungs, the brain and other bodily systems. At each point medical power is the sovereign power of a gaze that penetrates into bodies and which has the right to, as Bichat put it, 'open up a few corpses'.

This fascination with opening up corpses is not confined to medicine. In contemporary popular culture the corpse has become an object of obsessive concern, especially in terms of 'reading' the corpse. For example, there are the works of the American novelist Patricia Cornwell, with her pathologist heroine Dr Kay Scarpetta. There is also the success of the CBS television series *Crime Scene Investigation (CSI)*. This series focuses on the technology of crime scene investigation, and how forensic pathology can 'read' both crime scenes and bodies to determine the cause of death. The official web site for this show offers technical explanations of the devices by which crime scene investigators determine the cause of death, and the chance for visitors to the site to 'investigate' cases for themselves (with appropriately gruesome images). These are just two examples of how the penetration of the depths of the corpse is not only a matter for medical power but has become the means for us all to interrogate the time of death.

The crisis in the decision on the time of death that Agamben identifies with the new concept of brain death already seems to have its footing in the integration of death within medicine. We find in the early nineteenth-century clinic a series of medical decisions on the time of death that also gives us the concept of death as belonging to the individual and defining us. The capacity to make these decisions is the result of the availability of bare life within the clinic and the sovereign decision that defines that bare life, to use Agamben's terminology. The result is that in the space of the clinic the medical gaze becomes a sovereign power. This suggests the need to complicate Agamben's analysis to take into account these earlier developments. The dispersion of sovereign power through a symbiosis between the sovereign and the doctor has a longer history than Agamben recognises.

Another example of this exchange between medicine and sovereign power can be found in the early modern period. The literary historian Jonathan

Sawday describes the emergence of a 'culture of dissection' in this period, where medicine practises dissection on the body of the executed criminal. In this way, as he describes, medicine becomes part of the 'nexus of sovereignty' (Sawday, 1995: 80). The reason that it does so is that the dissection of the criminal's body is not simply about obtaining medical knowledge; instead it is the final ignominy visited on the body of the condemned. Medicine is completing the punishment dictated by the sovereign, and the anatomist becomes the final representative of sovereign power. The old power of death not only inflicted violent suffering and death, it also imposed the dissection of the body of the condemned. It tore that body into pieces in an act that was as much an act of power as an act of medicine.

This practice continued after the early modern period, with anatomists often stealing the corpses of those who had been executed. One, imaginary, example was described by the English novelist Samuel Richardson (1689–1761):

> And as soon as the poor creatures were half-dead, I was much surprised, before such a number of peace-officers, to see the populace fall to haling and pulling the carcasses with so much earnestness, as to occasion several warmer encounters, and broken heads. These, I was told, were the friends of the person executed, or such as, for the sake of tumult, chose to appear so, and some persons sent by private surgeons to obtain bodies for dissection. The contests between these were fierce and bloody, and frightful to look at. (Richardson, 1928: 219).

As we can see, Agamben ignores this history of the relationship between medicine and sovereignty constructed through acts of punishment and violence.

These absences suggest that the history of the intimate relationship between sovereign political power and medical power needs to be analysed over a longer duration. This is not to deny Agamben's assertion that the symbiosis of sovereign power and medical power has accelerated in the postwar period, but this symbiosis does not belong solely to that period. In trying to sketch the zone of indistinction into which we have plunged, Agamben underestimates how much more indistinct that zone is. As I mentioned in Chapter One, his history is too linear and not detailed enough to deal adequately with these problems. By privileging only certain historical events, such as the Nazi concentration camps and the inauguration of brain death, he risks downplaying a more refined and complicated historical, political and philosophical reading of modern death. In particular, more precision is required in tracing the spreading out of sovereign power behind various 'masks of power' and how medicine politicises death.

Another difficulty with Agamben's analysis of the relationship between medicine, power and death is an ambiguity in some of his arguments. At times, Agamben suggests that medicine works politically through 'pseudoscientific concepts' and 'pseudoscientific representations of the body, illness, and health' being used 'for ends of political control' (ME: 8). It appears, then, that the problem with medicine is that it is not properly scientific and, if it were, it would not be political. At other times, Agamben makes a more general argument which suggests that even when medicine is being scientific, such as in the situation concerning life-support technology, it still remains political. Is medicine only a problem when it is being unscientific, or is medicine as a science bound to political power?

THE SCIENCE OF DEATH

If the problem is with medicine's use of pseudoscientific concepts, then we might expect Agamben to provide us with some help in providing criteria for what is scientific and what is not; he does not. Also, is it only pseudoscientific concepts that can be used for political control? These are profoundly difficult questions, and we could consider the long and ongoing debate about the concepts of 'mental illness' for the extreme positions that can be taken on the 'reality' of mental illness and the political consequences of such positions. Another case, this time more 'securely' medical, would be that of the identification of AIDS as a disease entity and the effects this has had on immigration, citizenship status and treatment availability. I think that Agamben's use of the term 'pseudoscientific' creates more problems than he appears to recognise, not least because, as my second question suggests, it implies that scientific concepts are legitimate, as well as lacking any suggestion about how we might distinguish between scientific and pseudoscientific concepts. Agamben appears to have lost control of his rhetoric.

In *Homo Sacer* he clarifies his position somewhat when he argues that 'life and death are not properly scientific concepts but rather political concepts, which as such acquire a political meaning precisely only through a decision' (HS: 164). It is not so much that life and death are pseudoscientific concepts that can be used for political control, but that they are not properly scientific concepts and can only be defined through a political decision. Of course this is also a questionable assertion. Does it mean that if properly scientific concepts of life and death were found, which certainly could already be claimed, then death would cease to be political? I would suggest that it is more accurate to consider death as always political, and that Agamben's work helps to begin to substantiate this argument. Life and death are always a matter of a sovereign decision that decides on life and death through defining bare life.

This is why the 'medicalisation of death' is better understood as another sign of the politicisation of death. The power to decide on life and death, a political decision, passes from sovereign power as classically located in the head of state to the doctor as a new representative of that 'old power of death'. Then, with the controversy over brain death, that political decision is further fragmented between the medical and legal power to decide on death. Also, of course, there is then the involvement of others, such as priests, philosophers, patients' rights groups, etc. In each case it is not that sovereign power is weakening, becoming scientific or being made accountable; instead it is spreading. Through exploring how the decision on the time of death is a decision on bare life and how this decision takes place in the space of power of sovereignty, what is revealed is that the decision of the time of death is political, before any medical, biological or cultural meaning becomes attached to it.

It may well be that the attempt by death studies to consider the variations in the cultural and historical meanings of death is flawed, even when they are brought together with medical or biological meanings. What remains unthought is the political meaning of life and death, which is always the result of a sovereign decision. It is this 'meaning' I have tried to explore through considering modern death in terms of exposure. In fact, I shall suggest in my conclusion that to analyse death as exposure might well disrupt any 'meaning' of death, political or otherwise. Agamben's major failing, and why his work needs to be considered as a starting point, is that he does not consider the history of death and the specific ways in which the exposure to death, and to power, takes place. What he sets out to chart is a terrain that he regards as largely unexplored. While this is true, he underestimates the worth of previous explorations of the culture of death and so creates a limited narrative of modern death.

CONCLUSION: SURVIVAL OR SUICIDE?

To further chart the terrain of modern death, we must pursue the question of how we should respond to our exposure to death in modern culture. This is the question that will preoccupy us for the rest of this book. One of the forms of our exposure to death in modern culture is sustained survival that exposes us to extreme suffering, as we saw at the beginning of this chapter with the case of General Franco. This experience often takes place in the hospital room, and the success of medical dramas like the television series *ER* is evidence of our fascination with this exposure. What marks out *ER* from the long history of medical dramas on television is its production values, which approach those of the feature film. These include highly explicit representations of the suffering body and the speed of the show's storytelling and camerawork. This 'speed' mimics the rapid decision-making demanded in emergency room medicine, and gives the viewer a sense of the power of medicine to decide on life and death in a split second. Of course, though, despite their personal problems, the representation of the medical staff still tends to portray them as competent and caring, reassuring us about our vulnerability to medical power.

However, although we are fascinated by medical decision-making as 'drama', what seems to be lacking in the hospital room is any art of dying well – what was called, in the Middle Ages, the *ars moriendi*. Is, then, the only possible response to this drawn-out survival the desire to die? As Franco is recorded as saying 'how hard it is to die', must we then try to die if we are to be forced to survive? If we examine our modern culture of death in terms of this exposure to survival, it casts an interesting light on the preoccupation of modern culture with suicide. The French existentialist philosopher Albert Camus (1913–1960) began his book *The Myth of Sisyphus* (1955) with the claim that 'There is but one truly serious philosophical problem and that is suicide' (1975: 11). Ironically Camus would die in that most typical of modern ways: in a car crash. However, his posing of the problem of suicide as the fundamental problem could be seen not as the problem of the meaning of life, but as a result of our exposure to enforced survival by power.

In fact, existentialist philosophy was preoccupied with this problem of death. This philosophy had its heyday in the 1950s, which, as we saw, was the time of the new awareness of the threat of mass death in the wake of Hiroshima and Auschwitz. It posited a godless and irrational universe and stressed the importance of the individual decision as the act of freedom. What is interesting is that this act of freedom often took the form of suicide or murder. It was defined as a gratuitous act (*acte gratuit*), and the fact that such acts are gratuitous is a way of indicating the collapse of universal moral rules. If nothing is true, then everything is permitted, and the most extreme acts that become 'permitted' are suicide or murder. The first self-conscious literary description of such an act can be found in the French writer André Gide's 1914 novel *The Vatican Cellars* (1969). In that novel his anti-hero, Lafcadio, proves his 'freedom' by committing a random and motiveless murder, by pushing someone off a train.

We might see these sorts of acts not as proclamations of freedom in a world without moral rules but as failed attempts to master the unmasterable time of death and to escape the space of power.[3] They attempt to wrest control of the time of death from the invisible sovereign who haunts us at every turn. This is not to disregard the extreme pain and despair which often leads to suicide and the effects of this act on those left behind, nor is it an attempt to minimise or excuse the violence of murder and the destruction of human life. Instead it is to understand our fascination with these acts as a result of there being failed responses to our exposure to death in modern culture. These responses not only try to control the time of death but are also attempts to exit out of the time of enforced survival, most clearly with suicide. How can we evade the proliferating sovereign power that forces our survival, not least when it takes on the mask of the doctor? If we were to call for the right to end our medical treatment or for medically supervised euthanasia, then we would still remain within the space of medical power as the space of sovereign power. But to call for suicide appears to be hopeless, and also still remains within the space of the struggle over who holds the power of death. What we need are other possibilities of challenging our exposure to death.

NOTES

1. Foucault himself suffered a 'profane and banal' death due to AIDS-related illness. For a lurid account of Foucault's illness and supposed 'death wish' see Miller (1993).
2. There is an extensive literature on the problem of mourning. One of the most interesting examples is the collection of funeral addresses given by the French philosopher Jacques Derrida, called *The Work of Mourning* (2001).
3. The same could be said of the Fascist celebration of death, as in the slogan '*Viva la muerte!*' (Long live death!).

CHAPTER 4

Bioethics and Death

INTRODUCTION: WHAT IS BIOETHICS?

Bioethics is a relatively new academic discipline that aims to apply philosophy to practical ethical issues raised by health care and the biological sciences. It developed as a separate discipline during the 1960s, and was prompted by concerns about the growing power of doctors and the dilemmas posed by new technological developments in medicine. As the name suggests it is an ethics focused on issues of life, and because of this concern it also has to deal with the boundary between life and death, especially with issues like euthanasia. Another question that it has focused on is the one I discussed in the previous chapter: how we should decide whether to continue offering life-support to patients who will never regain consciousness. In their introduction to *A Companion to Bioethics* Helga Kuhse and Peter Singer explain how bioethics treats this question as '*an ethical decision*, on which patients and others may have views no less defensible than those of doctors' (1998: 3, my emphasis). While Agamben points out that the medical decision on death is actually a political decision and must be contested politically, Kuhse and Singer put their faith in ethics as a means of challenging medical power.

This 'ethical turn' is problematic for two reasons. The first is that in treating medical decisions ethically these sorts of approaches obscure the political context of modern death. In the previous three chapters I have sketched the political dimension of our exposure to death generally and in modern culture in particular. Why is it so difficult to recognise that modern culture involves this politics of death? The difficulty may well be that as bare life becomes the basis of all political identity it becomes more difficult to distinguish it. It is as if we stand too close to bare life to really see what lies before us, or, to be more precise, within us. While bioethics responds to this situation, and tries to contest medical power, it only does so ethically and ignores, or downplays, this political dimension. The second problem is that, when bioethics treats these decisions as ethical matters that it is competent to comment on, it too is taking on the role of sovereign power in deciding on death. As we saw in the previous chapter, philosophers and others play new roles in the decision on death, but this does not mean the limitation or the end of death as an issue of political power. Instead the bioethicist may be taking up the 'mask of power'.

It does appear that medical power is extending itself further into our bodies, especially with the new technologies of genetic manipulation and the mapping of the human genome. This means that some critique of medical power is becoming more and more urgent. The question is whether bioethics can provide us with this. In this chapter we shall examine how bioethics attempts to contest medical power and suggest some difficulties with this 'ethical turn'. What Agamben will argue is that we need to radically revise our ethics if we are to come to terms with our exposure to death in modern culture. The danger of bioethics is that, in turning these issues into subjects to be decided on ethically, it will leave this situation untouched. Also, which is even more dangerous, it may end up even ratifying the intrusion of power into our bodies by turning these intrusions into matters for ethical debate. In doing so it would fail to be properly ethical because it has not properly analysed the problem of life. This would be ironic for a discourse that is, supposedly, an ethics of life (*bioethics*).

My approach to these questions obviously involves criticisms of bioethics, but it must also be stressed that bioethics is a heterogeneous and evolving discourse that is not always insensitive to the political problem of modern death. What is also important about bioethics it that it aims at a practical confrontation with medical power. I first consider one example of how bioethics constructs an ethics of modern death around precisely the same issues with which Agamben engages: the decision to withhold the use of life-support technologies and the definition of death. Then I explore the more general problem of the 'ethical turn' in contemporary philosophy and how this is played out in the realm of biomedicine. Here the work of the contemporary French philosopher Alain Badiou is vital, as he provides the most compelling critique of modern ethics as nothing more than an 'ethical ideology' in which human beings are reduced to 'the status of victim, of suffering beast, of emaciated, dying body' (Badiou, 2001: 11). However, Badiou's own attempt to save us from this fate and to resituate human beings in their proper dimension of truth is also problematic. Therefore, we must turn to Agamben's own attempt to resolve this problem. In the third volume of *Homo Sacer*, called *Remnants of Auschwitz*, we find an attempt to found a new ethics that tries to answer the production of bare life by sovereign power.

The ethics of life often depends on thinking of the human being as 'subject', whether as a philosophical subject, a political subject or an ethical subject. Contemporary critical theory has been dominated by the question of the death of the subject: in the 1960s Michel Foucault's announced the 'death of man', Roland Barthes announced the death of the author, Louis Althusser called for a 'theoretical anti-humanism' and Jacques Lacan criticised 'ego-psychology'. Since then there have been many attempts to return to the subject or to recover the subject from the attacks. The question of the ethics of life and death allows us a different, and perhaps more productive, approach to the death, and possible return, of the subject. This 'death' is no longer treated as metaphorical and so it is possible to reconfigure what is at stake for ethics, politics, philosophy and our own existence in the modern culture of death. These debates, which have often seemed abstract, take on a far more pressing sense when they involve questions of literal life and death. This also allows us to resituate these debates in the practical, where they belong.

THE ETHICS OF MODERN DEATH

Agamben argues that 'What is left unquestioned in the contemporary debates on bioethics and biopolitics, in fact, is precisely what would deserve to be questioned before anything else, that is, the very biological concept of life' (ME: 7); this is not completely true. One contributor to the debate on bioethics places the issue of life at the centre of his deliberations, the Australian philosopher Peter Singer (b. 1946). Singer is among the best known and most widely read of contemporary philosophers, as well as being one of the most provocative and controversial. His most well-known work has been on the issue of the mistreatment of animals by human beings, but he has also engaged in the analysis of the bioethics of life and death. In fact these issues are linked for Singer because his work is involved in a questioning of what life is. He has not shied away from the controversial implications of his work, such as that a great ape would have more right to life than a severely disabled human infant. In the field of bioethics his central argument is that we need to replace what he calls the 'sanctity of life ethic' with a new 'quality of life ethic', a task which involves 'unsanctifying human life' (Singer, 2002).

Although Singer is not a particularly typical example of a bioethical philosopher, he is useful to consider because he does not shy away from the radical conclusions his work implies. As Slavoj Zizek remarks: 'One cannot dismiss Singer as a monstrous exaggeration – what Adorno said about psychoanalysis (that its truth resides in its very exaggerations) fully holds for Singer: he is so traumatic and intolerable because his scandalous "exaggerations" directly render visible the truth of so-called postmodern ethics' (in Zizek and Dolar, 2002: 143). His new 'quality of life' ethic reveals, for Zizek, the 'Darwinian' nature of postmodern ethics in which the species is divided into those worthy of ethical consideration and those not; ethics becomes a field of 'biological' struggle. The paradox is that because he is so untypical, by fearlessly drawing his conclusions from his premises, he is actually the most typical bioethical philosopher. He is unafraid to reveal what others working in the field might prefer to leave implicit or unspoken. In particular, it is his radical critique of the traditional sanctity of life ethic that forces us to face the consequences of problems that other bioethical philosophers may have minimised.

To understand the transition from the sanctity of life ethic to the quality of life ethic, Singer takes up and compares the responses of the medical and legal authorities in the US and Britain to two cases of patients in a persistent vegetative state (PVS) whose parents requested the withdrawal of life-support. PVS is defined by the latest edition of the *Oxford Concise Medical Dictionary* as 'the condition of living like a vegetable, without consciousness or the ability to initiate voluntary action, as a result of brain damage'

(Martin, 2003: 524).[1] The first case, which we have already encountered in the previous chapter, is that of Karen Ann Quinlan. In 1976 Karen Quinlan was in what was then described as a 'permanent coma' and what is now called PVS. Her doctors were of the opinion that she would never recover and in this state she was kept alive by a respirator that maintained her breathing. As Karen Quinlan's parents were Roman Catholics they could not accept any active termination of their daughter's life, but they were advised by a priest that a respirator was an 'extraordinary means' to sustain life. While it would be deliberate killing to withdraw 'ordinary means' of life-support, to withdraw 'extraordinary means' was not problematic. However, the doctors refused this request and the case went to court. The case initially turned on this distinction between the means to sustain life. For the court-appointed guardian the central issue was whether it was right to cause the death of another human being. On the other hand, the Roman Catholic Bishop of New Jersey, Bishop Casey, argued that as the respirator was an extraordinary means of treatment the decision to withdraw it by Karen's parents was 'morally correct' (in Singer, 1994: 71).

As Singer points out this distinction between 'ordinary' and 'extraordinary' means of treatment is extremely fragile, if not unsustainable. The obvious question is why is a piece of common medical apparatus 'extraordinary'? Also, even if it is, why is this ground to withdraw its use as opposed to 'ordinary' treatments? In the face of these issues Singer's suggestion is that we concede that what is really being made here is a decision on quality of life and that we live with the ethical consequences of this. The very description of the respirator as an 'extraordinary means' of sustaining life depends on our already having decided that it is not worthwhile sustaining the life of a patient in this state. If Karen had a reasonable hope of recovery no one would object to the use of a respirator, but because she does not then it becomes an 'extraordinary' means of treatment. If she had a reasonable quality of life with a respirator, if she were conscious and able to enjoy a range of activities, then again its use would not be 'extraordinary'. This use of the word 'extraordinary' simply disguises the fact that what is really being made is a decision based on quality of life.

In Singer's words this distinction is just a 'fig leaf' to protect the sanctity of life ethic when the intention is that Karen Ann Quinlan should die. At the first trial the judgement was that Karen should not die. It took the decision of the New Jersey Supreme Court, which held there was a constitutional right to privacy that allowed the family of a dying incompetent patient to withdraw 'artificial life support systems', to lead to the withdrawal of Karen's respirator. However, in another case of PVS, this 'fig leaf' between 'ordinary' and 'extraordinary' means of treatment was abandoned. The consequence was that the sanctity of life ethic was abandoned in favour of an open admission of a new quality of life ethic. This new quality of life ethic granted the right to deliberately end the life of a patient in certain circumstances.

THE END OF THE SANCTITY OF LIFE ETHIC

The case concerned a young man called Anthony Bland. In 1989 he became a victim of the worst disaster in British sporting history when he went to see his soccer team, Liverpool, play Nottingham Forest in an FA Cup semifinal at Hillsborough Football Stadium in Sheffield. At the start of the match a fatal crush occurred in which supporters were pushed against fencing put up to prevent them getting on the field; ninety-five people died and Anthony Bland was so deprived of oxygen that when he reached hospital it was found that only his brain stem had survived. Peter Singer quotes Lord Justice Hoffman's description of Anthony Bland's terrible condition:

> Since April 15 1989 Anthony Bland has been in persistent vegetative state. He lies in Airedale General Hospital in Keighley, fed liquid food by a pump passing through his nose and down the back of his throat into the stomach. His bladder is emptied through a catheter inserted through his penis, which from time to time has caused infections requiring dressing and antibiotic treatment. His stiffened joints have caused his limbs to be rigidly contracted so that his arms are tightly flexed across his chest and his legs unnaturally contorted. Reflex movements in his throat cause him to vomit and dribble. Of all this, and the presence of members of his family who take turns to visit him, Anthony Bland has no consciousness at all. The parts of his brain which provided him with consciousness have turned to fluid. The darkness and oblivion which descended at Hillsborough will never depart. His body is alive, but he has no life in the

sense that even the most pitifully handicapped but conscious human being has a life. But the advances of modern medicine permit him to be kept in this state for years, even perhaps for decades. (In Singer, 1994: 58)

Such a fate is almost unimaginable, as are the effects it had on Anthony Bland's family and carers. He has been left in the state of what Singer calls 'mere biological existence' (1994: 80).

The usual medical practice in such cases is for the doctors to withdraw artificial feeding, in which case the patient dies in a week or two. However, in this case the coroner in Sheffield was inquiring into the deaths caused by the Hillsborough disaster. When Anthony's doctor informed the coroner of his intention to withdraw artificial feeding the coroner warned him that he could be at risk of criminal charges, perhaps even being charged with murder. Therefore the administrator of the hospital in which Anthony Bland was being cared for applied to the Family Division of the High Court for permission to lawfully discontinue medical treatment 'except for the sole purpose of enabling Anthony Bland to end his life and to die peacefully with the greatest dignity and the least distress' (in Singer, 1994: 60). The Official Solicitor, a public law officer, was appointed guardian for Bland at the Family Division. He opposed the withdrawal of treatment on the grounds that it was, legally, murder. The presiding judge of the Family Division did not accept this argument and an appeals process ensued which led to the case being heard before the House of Lords, the highest court in the British judicial system.

The decision of the British courts was based around the question of the patient's best interests. As the treatment that Anthony Bland received brought him no benefit there was no need to continue treatment simply to sustain biological life. In the House of Lords Lord Mustill stated that 'the pitiful state of Anthony Bland and the suffering of his devoted family must attract the sympathy of all' (in Singer, 1994: 64). Therefore the judges sought a solution that would bring an end to the situation in which there was no hope for Anthony Bland or his family. However, Singer points out that this decision broke new ethical ground in two crucial respects: first, considerations of the quality of life entered into the decision on sustaining life and, secondly, it was accepted that it was a lawful course to allow the death of an innocent human being. The result is that this case meant the end, at least in the British courts, of the sanctity of life ethic. If we follow the traditional interpretation of the sanctity of human life, then all human lives are of equal value. As Mr Justice Vincent, a judge of the Supreme Court of Victoria, Australia, put it in 1986, 'the law does not permit decisions to be made concerning the quality of life nor any assessment of the value of any human being' (in Singer, 1994: 65). It was this fundamental legal and ethical principle that was overturned in the series of judgements made by a total of nine judges on the case of Anthony Bland.

Singer gathers together the statements made by the judges, at different stages of the legal process, which each make clear that the judges did not see life in the biological sense as valuable in itself. If we focus on the final decision made by the judges in the House of Lords, the view was that, as Lord Goff put it, 'it is not in the interests of an insentient patient to continue the life-supporting care and treatment' (in Singer, 1994: 67). The Law Lords did not regard mere biological existence as always of value; instead, 'life' must involve some capacity for awareness or conscious experience. This, then, was one result of the legal decision of the House of Lords; the other was to confront the issue of lawfully ending the life of an innocent human being. If Anthony Bland's life lacked value, then the decision to withhold care from him would mean the deliberate decision to end his life. The previous view had been that a doctor could relieve pain and suffering even if that would incidentally shorten a patient's life, but that no doctor, or any other person, had the right to end life.

While in the Karen Quinlan case the 'fig leaf' of a distinction between ordinary and extraordinary means of treatment was maintained to justify withdrawing treatment, this now disappeared. The British House of Lords was open that the decision to withdraw treatment intended the death of the patient. Death was no longer treated as some sort of side-effect of withdrawing treatment, but as something lawfully intended. The judges did not simply dismiss the traditional ethic of the sanctity of human life but they found it outweighed by the issue of the quality of life. Of course, it could be argued that this leaves the sanctity of life ethic substantially intact, except in such exceptional cases as that of Anthony Bland. However, the sanctity of life ethic is clear that it is never permissible to intentionally take

an innocent human life, and that it is an absolute principle. So the judges
have, in fact, decided to take up the new ethic of the quality of life.

Does this decision permit euthanasia? The Law Lords thought not
because they drew a distinction between actively seeking to end life, which
would be euthanasia, and ending life by not providing treatment, as in the
case of Anthony Bland. This distinction between acts (directly bringing
about death) and omissions (causing death by not acting) proved difficult
to sustain. For Singer this difficulty is the opening to 'a new approach to
life-and-death decisions' (1994: 80), which admits the need for a new ethics
that can better confront the problems that new medical technologies and the
old sanctity of life ethic have left us with. Instead of seeing this new ethics
as a matter of redefining death, Singer sees it as a matter of defining life in
terms of the quality of life. Rather than constantly shifting the boundary
between life and death to permit medical intervention or to decide that a
patient is 'really' dead, as happened with the concept of brain death, we
should, instead, define what we mean by life. We need to admit that our
ethics permits the ending of life, the removal of organs from the living and
experimentation on the living. To define life we must concentrate on what
makes life of value, and 'focus on ethically relevant characteristics like the
capacity for enjoyable experiences, for interacting with others, or for having
preferences about continued life' (Singer, 1994: 192).

PROBLEMS WITH THE QUALITY OF LIFE ETHIC

This is the heart of Singer's 'revolution' in ethics: from an ethics that treats
all life as sacred and of equal worth to a new quality of life ethic that
decides which lives have value and which do not. His work may not be
representative of bioethics as a whole but it is a *bio*ethics: an ethics of life.
There are several problems with this new ethics of life, which are closely
related to our exposure to death by medical power in modern culture. These
problems will be listed briefly and then explored in more detail. First, Singer's
argument that there are human lives which have value and those which do
not is dangerously close to the distinction made by the Nazis between life
and 'life unworthy of being lived'. Secondly, Singer's confident dismissal of

the importance of 'mere biological existence' mimics the exclusion of bare life that is the sign of the operation of sovereign power. Thirdly, his concept of the 'old' ethic of the sacredness of life lacks any understanding of how sacred life is defined through exposure to death, that is, through the 'quality' of life. This means that it is impossible to easily distinguish between the old ethic of sacred life and the new ethic of quality of life. Fourthly, and finally, Singer's ethics of life obscure the politics of life in modern culture.

1. The historian Michael Burleigh (1994) has demonstrated how the Nazi programme of 'euthanasia' for the mentally ill and the disabled involved the medical administration of judgements on the value of life that led to mass murder. As Singer puts faith in the medical profession to administer his ethics of quality of life, it is no surprise that his work has proved controversial in Germany, leading to the so-called 'Singer debate' on euthanasia. Although Singer's work cannot be understood as a new version of this Nazi politics of life, he certainly cavalierly ignores this history. The exposure of life that was found under Nazism has not disappeared in the postwar democracies, due to the fact that bare life is still, and even more so, the ground of our political identities. This means that a great deal more caution would need to be exercised when considering quality of life issues than Singer realises. His choice of extreme cases can make the issue seem clear-cut, but, as history has shown us again and again, the definition of life as not fully human or as disposable is often not. Instead the definition of life as 'unworthy of life' is highly politicised, as the case of Nazi Germany and other state racisms make clear. Although Singer wants to contest medical power and make it subject to ethical debate, his ethics of quality of life is historically naïve.

2. Singer's confident dismissal of 'mere biological existence' as not actual life is profoundly problematic, and establishes a further disturbing parallel with the Nazi politics of life and death. In Chapter Two we saw how the Nazi camps created a form of life that was reduced to mere biological existence: the camp inmate reduced to the state of the 'Muslim'. By Singer's criteria of 'quality of life' there would, it seems, be no reason to preserve these individuals. What Agamben shows, and what Singer ignores, is that mere biological existence, life exposed to death, is not defined by science so much as politics. The decision on life and death depends on defining

someone as bare life, as mere biological existence, which is what then exposes them to death. Instead of the quality of life ethic offering us a new ethics, it seems to offer an ethics that goes along with the operation of sovereign power and which cannot resist or contest it. Both the ethic of the quality of life and power agree that mere biological existence is no real form of life but only life totally vulnerable to disposal.

3. When Singer talks about the old ethics of the sacredness of life, he does not realise how that ethic also involved a decision on the quality of life as well. This threatens his whole distinction between these two forms of ethics. The sacredness is defined through the exposure of the body to power and to the threat of death. It is the sacred man who may be killed and yet not sacrificed, the man who is produced as bare life. This means that the 'old' ethics of the sacredness of life also rests on a decision defining the quality of life, by producing the sacred politically as that which is abandoned. The ethics of life as sacred did not involve preserving all life equally, but involved taking a decision of what would count as life and what could be left to die. Singer does not seem to realise that this problem has always been central to Western culture. Therefore, his 'new' ethics of the quality of life is not so new, and it may obscure the issue of life as sacred that it is supposed to solve or replace.

4. The final point, one which summarises these previous problems, is that Singer cannot grasp the political constitution of life and death. He turns to bioethics to limit and regulate medical power, without considering the political issues. This is all the more ironic as Singer regards bioethics as emerging out of the political protests of the 1960s against abuses of power, such as the civil rights movement, feminism and the protests against the Vietnam War. However, he does not suggest a politics of life and death but an ethics instead. In this way his work is part of the zone of indistinction into which bare life and sovereign power have plunged in modern culture. His bioethics takes up the role of sovereign power in making the decision on life and death in the name of ethics. But it remains political, and sovereign power might have found a new mask: the bioethicist. Despite his political claims about bioethics his work leads to the depoliticisation of life and death and a failure to engage with our exposure to death in modern culture. Does this mean we must abandon the hope of any ethics of life and death?

ETHICS AS IDEOLOGY

The contemporary French philosopher Alain Badiou (b. 1937) has made the most scathing critique of the ethical turn in modern thought, and of bioethics in particular. Badiou is an ex-Maoist radical who has developed a new militant philosophy of truth.[2] In his book *Ethics: An Essay on the Understanding of Evil* (2001) he attacks the way in which ethics has become the dominant ideology of our times. He regards the turn to ethics as a result of the collapse of any genuinely political thinking and engagement. Instead of this new ideology of ethics being a challenge to power it is actually compatible with the existing order. The emphasis of ethics on human rights and the rights of the individual does not help liberate the individual from power but reinforces the arrogance of Western individualism. Why does this new ethics fail to be ethical?

The problem of this 'new' discourse of ethics is that it is based on the individual as the ethical subject and the assumptions it makes about this individual. For Badiou there are four main presuppositions that ethical ideology makes. First, it tries to identify a general human subject. This general subject can play two roles, either it is the suffering victim, who must be rescued, or it is the ethical subject, who can judge the suffering of others. Secondly, ethical discourse replaces politics and tries to suggest that any radical political project leads to disaster. This is linked to the third assumption of ethical ideology: evil is the primary problem. It assumes that there is evil and suffering in the world, which it is the job of ethics to relieve. Any political project that tries to eliminate evil is seen as always only leading to more evil. Although ethics claims to try and deal with evil, it presumes that evil is eternal, and so always depends on the existence of evil. Fourthly, it defines the rights of the individual as the right to avoid evil, to avoid interference. Instead of any positive programme, ethical ideology depends on the negative concept that we be left alone and the rights that it proclaims are negative rights.

The major problem of ethical ideology, which will link to the problem of bioethics, is that it defines human beings as victims, or as suffering animals, which it is the role of the ethical to save. Therefore, ethics depends on bare life, or, to use the terminology I have adopted, it depends on our exposure to death. In this ethical ideology evil always comes first, and we can define the individual through their suffering. We know what a human being is, we know when a human being suffers, and a human being has the right to be relieved of his or her suffering. It is also our ethical duty to undertake whatever measures are required to relieve that suffering. This discourse, which is based on the individual, based on the idea of the human subject, does not lead to any radical resistance to power. Instead it leads to the pessimistic acceptance of the status quo.

Badiou's tendency to dismiss the issue of human rights in such a blanket fashion is problematic. While it is true that such rights can reinforce this image of the human being as victim, they can also offer resources for resistance. What Badiou does make clear is the danger that ethics might not so much oppose misery and death, which it takes as its starting point, as feed off them. In fact, he argues that ethics is arrogant enough to decide who should die and who should be saved in the face of this evil. When it does so, ethics takes up the power over life and death to decide who is the deserving victim requiring aid and who is undeserving and should be left to die. This raises disturbing questions about the ethical turn in contemporary thought and, especially, the turn to bioethics. For Badiou ethics is hypocritical because, although it proclaims its abhorrence of evil, it actually depends on thinking that 'the only thing that can really happen to someone is death' (2001: 35). He is particularly suspicious of the rise of bioethics, which he regards as an ethics of death and not of life.

THE IDEOLOGY OF BIOETHICS

What bioethics tends towards is the administration of death: that is, when it discusses issues such as euthanasia or the withdrawal of life-support, it tends to treat suffering and death as pre-given matters to be decided upon. It makes no real attempt to question what we might mean by suffering, dying or old age and, instead, administers socially accepted ideas of 'valuable' life or life 'without value'. In fact, bioethics strives, as we have seen in the case of Peter Singer, to define happiness and life but this leaves death outside its thinking. Worse than this, it can even become fascinated with death as the limit of its thinking. In this way 'mere biological existence', life exposed to death, is what fascinates bioethics but also what it can never analyse or account for.

Badiou makes the connection between bioethics and the state politics of Nazism. He argues that the Nazi politics of life is, fundamentally, an ethics of life that permits putting to death in the name of the value of life. Therefore the appearance of state commissions of bioethics today belongs to this dangerous legacy. These commissions make similar decisions on the value of life, not in terms of racist ideology but in terms of economic efficiency. The allocation of health care has become an economic matter, with the so-called 'ethical' debates actually focused on the costs of certain forms of care. In the case of patients on life-support we have seen how the issue of the economic 'burden' these patients place on health care providers has been an element in the redefinition of death. These economic decisions are also often determined by questions of nationality and citizenship. Those that lead 'productive' lives are seen as more valuable than those who are defined as a 'drain' on the resources of the state. Anyone who doesn't properly 'belong' to the national community is somehow not 'worthy' of proper health care.

When doctors come to make life-and-death decisions they may well ponder the ethical implications of their actions. However, this 'ethical ideology' conceives the sick and ill as passive objects of discussion, subject to the decision-making power of doctors and bureaucrats. What bioethics cannot consider is that these individuals may not simply be victims to be saved, or not, by the power of medicine. It is an ethics of pity that erases the problem of the needs of the specific individual, despite references often being made to the rights of the individual. As we saw in Chapter One, these rights are based on bare life, on life exposed to death, and do not adequately question how life becomes defined as bare life. Ethics is an abstract ideology that cannot properly deal with the concrete issues posed by suffering and death, except by creating some general rule about which lives are worth saving and which are not. Badiou goes as far as arguing that 'The conjunction of "ethics" and "bio" is *in itself* threatening' (2001: 37).

To attack this ethical ideology we have to realise that there is no need for ethics. What the doctor must do is treat each individual patient according to their need and disregard issues of their citizenship, their productivity, of how 'worthy' they are of life (Badiou, 2001: 15). The problem is that Badiou's rule is itself quite abstract. His 'clinical' ethics demands that doctors treat their patients to the limits of what they can do, despite the consequences. We might argue that this is problematic in the case of patients with PVS, for example. Here, they would continue to be sustained but are they actually living life at all? Although Badiou might be right in criticising how medicine and bioethics define life in terms of existing social criteria of worth, he does not really confront the ethical problems posed by these extreme cases. What is valuable about his criticisms is that they call attention to the nature of specific cases and the limit of any abstract ethical rule making. They also draw attention to how ethics often smuggles in political assumptions and remains in a close relationship with power.

In his book on ethics Badiou goes further in trying to construct a new ethic of truths that will counter ethical ideology.[3] Badiou's description of his ethics is, however, rather slippery. On the one hand, he talks about a general ethics of dealing with a situation according to the demands of that specific situation, and this includes dealing with the demands the patient makes on the doctor in the clinic. On the other hand, Badiou suggests that we only really face ethical situations when we are faced by events that set in motion the process of truth. These events include scientific discoveries, political revolutions, new artistic innovations and falling in love. They are all exceptional moments and do not belong in common situations. His ethic of truths, real ethics we could say, only happens when we are called on to be ethical by an event. This is the first problem of his new ethics, that it falls between dealing with situations according to their specific demands and responding to exceptional events. Badiou never really explains the connection between the two, or the reason for these two ethical 'levels'.

A second problem occurs in his new ethics when we are called on to be faithful to an exceptional event. This is the ethical moment and in it, for Badiou, we must go beyond our animal nature, beyond our finite mortal being, and enter into the process of sustaining truth. Although our suffering animal being is the foundation, it is surpassed as we compose ourselves as a subject of truth. Badiou's ethical subject is a subject who supports and maintains a fidelity to the truth process initiated by an event. The problem is that this subject, who is 'subject to truth', to use Peter Hallward's phrase, has to set aside their animal existence. Although this subject is founded on our 'animal' existence, and Badiou stresses the importance of this biological level, it is still subsidiary to the process of truth. This means that, while Badiou powerfully criticises existing ethics, his own ethics risks abandoning bare life as well. If bare life is our mere biological existence, our suffering and exposure to death, then leaving aside this animal existence is exactly the same act as that of sovereign power.

In his rush to avoid the tendency of ethical ideology to think of human beings as suffering victims, Badiou actually abandons the problem of suffering and bare life. His own gesture, which is designed to give us a new philosophy and ethics of truth, rests on the 'inclusive exclusion' of bare life, and so repeats the gesture of power. In his ethic of truths, inclusive exclusion takes place because our animal existence is included in the process of truth, as its foundation, but it is excluded, because it does not belong to truth. The paradox is that Badiou can provide us with a scathing critique of the limits of ethics, and of bioethics in particular, but that his own ethics does not resolve the problem of our exposure to death in modern culture. Instead, we will need to try and create a new ethics that does not depend on abandoning bare life. Is it possible to construct an ethics that begins from mere biological existence? Do we have to always abandon bare life, as both Singer and Badiou do, to construct an ethics? These questions can only be answered if we return to the situation of life exposed to death in its most extreme forms, if we return to the concentration camps.

ETHICS AFTER AUSCHWITZ

This is precisely the task Agamben undertakes in his book *Remnants of Auschwitz* (1999). It begins with the problem of bearing witness to what happened in the camps. If the camps are the most unbearable and extreme situations of human suffering, then how can anyone who has survived the camps describe what has happened? Especially since the survivors, because they have survived, have not witnessed the extremes of degradation and death faced by those who did not. This is the problem that has tortured many Holocaust survivors. The Italian writer Primo Levi (1919–1987), who survived Auschwitz, has written 'At a distance of years one can today definitely affirm that the history of the Lagers [the camps] has been written almost exclusively by those who, like myself, never fathomed them to the bottom' (1988: 6). It is this problem of witnessing that leads Agamben to challenge the attempts to construct ethics after Auschwitz.

The event of Auschwitz demands that one witness what happened there but the unbearable nature of that event is also what prevents witnessing, so 'the survivors bear witness to something it is impossible to bear witness to' (RA: 13). What we find in Auschwitz that is so unbearable is, according to Agamben, life reduced to mere biological existence. This can be found in the terrible experience of the *Muselmann* or 'Muslim', who is reduced by starvation and suffering to the state of a living death. No one can bear the sight of the 'Muslim'. Agamben describes a film shot immediately after the liberation of Bergen-Belsen concentration camp in 1945 which dwells on the sight of thousands of naked corpses piled in graves. Since the film is attempting to offer proof of what happened in this camp, no detail is spared. However, at one point the camera captures the sight of those reduced to the state of *Muselmänner* ('Muslims') or very close to it. These images last only a few seconds before the cameraman draws away from them to return to the corpses: they are more bearable than the sight of living death.

Even in the camps the 'Muslims' were left excluded, as outside the gaze of both the SS and the other camp inmates. As the one study solely devoted to the 'Muslims' reports, 'For the prisoners who collaborated, the Muslims were a source of anger and worry; for the SS, they were merely useless garbage. Every group thought only about eliminating them, each in its own way' (Ryn and Klodzinski in RA: 43). If any ethics is to be truly ethical, then it must be an ethics that bears witness to the 'Muslim' and which does not repeat this failure to witness the unbearable. Any ethics that excludes mere biological existence will fail the 'test' of ethics after Auschwitz. Not only would it exclude those suffering that fate today, it would also exclude the suffering of those camp inmates.

If we were to create an ethics based on the dignity of human life, then this ethics would risk leaving outside it those who have been reduced to these levels of degradation. To speak of dignity or respect in the face of the

'Muslim' is to exclude these individuals from consideration as human. If the dignity of life is not an appropriate response, then neither is any invoking of the dignity of death. The new horror that we find in the camps is that not only is life completely degraded, but so also is death. The tendency has been to see this degradation of death as another example of the general degradation of death in modern culture. However, Agamben insists that what we find in the 'Muslim' is the collapse of any attempt to distinguish between a proper or 'improper' death, death with dignity or death without. What happens in the camps ruins these sorts of distinctions. As such, when we try to face the 'Muslim', we face the limits of our ethics, and our ethical categories are thrown into crisis.

For example, if we were to put our faith in an ethics based on communication, as does the German social theorist Jürgen Habermas (b. 1929), then this too could not deal with the situation of the 'Muslim'. Habermas states that our ethics comes from our capacity to communicate with others, and the agreements we enter into when we communicate. These agreements ensure a commitment to truth and shared communication, which underpin this ethics of communication. However, the 'Muslim' has been reduced to the state of being unable to speak and being outside communication. Does this mean that because they cannot communicate they should remain outside ethics? If we define ethics in terms of dignity or in terms of language, then the 'Muslim' is excluded. Instead, we must construct a new ethics that begins from this extreme form of bare life. This new ethics is 'an ethics of a form of life that begins where dignity ends' (RA: 69). There is life even, or especially, in the most extreme degradation.

What is Agamben's new ethics of a bare life that begins where dignity ends? To find this new ethics he turns to the experience of shame which has been felt by the survivors of the death camps. This shame is the result of having survived, of having been one of the saved and not one of the drowned, to use Primo Levi's distinction. It is also the shame of not being the 'Muslim' and the shame felt before those who were. Although Agamben begins with this particular sort of shame, he goes on to argue that shame is what creates our experience of subjectivity. To become a subject, to become human, is to feel shame. What we feel in this experience of shame is the sense of our own existence as bare life, our shame before our own disorder and oblivion. What we witness when we become a subject is the ruin of any secure sense of being a subject; we witness the fact that we are only mere biological existence. It is also out of this experience of shame that we can face the problem of bearing witness to the 'Muslim', who is the figure of this extreme degradation and the oblivion of the subject.

The subject is not a subject due to some ethical addition that removes or distinguishes them from bare life, but we are subjects because we feel shame. This experience of shame is neither about the death of the subject nor about some return to the subject as ground. Instead, what we find is that our subjectivity is 'based' on the movement of desubjectification, of our becoming or witnessing our bare life as extreme degradation. What Agamben's new ethics does is begin from the shame felt in witnessing the 'Muslim' to argue that this opens up a more general experience of shame before bare life. Although the 'Muslim' is the extreme example of degradation, we all feel shame before the fact that we are constituted as subjects through abandoning the bare life within us. There is a kind of fissure or gap between our capacities as speaking beings, as subjects, and our living being, the fact that we are also bare life.

The problem with previous attempts to found ethics is that they tend to repeat the exclusion of the living being in favour of the speaking being. They try to preserve and maintain some distinct ethical element, which is what makes us truly ethical, but this element is built on and excludes bare life. The same effect takes place in Singer's work and Badiou's, which both exclude mere biological existence in different ways. Agamben's new ethics, in contrast, seeks out shame as the 'non-place' between the speaking being and the living being. How does this situation allow us to bear witness to the 'Muslim'? What we must recognise is that the 'Muslim', as the absolute biological remnant of the living being, cannot be separated from the survivor, as the speaking being who speaks for the 'Muslim'. Instead, in each of us there is this strange experience of articulation between the living being and the speaking being. Any ethics after Auschwitz must maintain this inseparable articulation of the two together, and maintain the sense of shame that it brings, unless it wants to repeat the exclusion of the 'Muslim'.

This allows us a response to power that exposes us to death, or exposes us to survival always on the verge of death. What power produces when it produces the 'Muslim' is someone left as a biological remnant or leftover, which cannot be witnessed. It separates out bare life as survival from any possibility of speech or identity. This isolation of pure bare life, pure survival, creates a subject who is totally exposed to death while being denied the 'release' of death. Through this isolation and stripping away of identity and the creation of the 'remnant', power saturates bare life completely. How can Agamben's new ethics counter this attempt to separate off the 'Muslim' as the remnant? His new ethics insists on the survival of the 'Muslim' as a remnant as providing the possibility of our responding to this exposure to death. As the 'remnant', as the one who is violently deprived of his or her humanity, the survival of the 'Muslim' in this state allows us to witness the fact that *the one whose humanity is completely destroyed is the one who is truly human* (RA: 133).

Agamben is arguing that there is no human essence except in our capacity to be destroyed. What makes us human is what makes us vulnerable to this radical exposure to life that is only 'death in motion'. Therefore the only real basis of ethics lies in this experience of our exposure to power and to being held on the verge of death. Modern ethics can only be modern if it measures up to the experience of the exposure to death in modern culture. Agamben's new ethics tries to do this by insisting that we always carry the shame of bare life and that this shame forces us to witness the impossibility of ever separating off completely bare life, as power would like to do. His ethical 'subject' is the subject who bears witness to the fact that they find themselves only in the oblivion of losing their subjectivity. What power constantly strives to do is to break the connection between the living and speaking being by isolating bare life as survival. Agamben returns to this experience of survival and finds in it the possibility of an ethics that can refuse to separate off survival.

This new ethics is found in the remnant, and in survival. What we find in Auschwitz, according to Agamben, is the attempt to produce an absolute separation of bare life. We must witness this attempt but refuse it through an act of witnessing that always maintains our connection to bare life. Ethics after Auschwitz will be an ethics that refuses to exclude bare life, and an ethics that bears witness to the irreducible disjunction between the living being and the speaking being. How does such an ethics help us to answer the problems which biomedicine poses for us today? It seems, unlike bioethics or Badiou's 'ethic of truths', to offer no solutions to these pressing problems. However, what it does offer is the insistence that for any ethics to be truly ethical it must not simply exclude bare life as what is not ethical. It turns existing ethical discourse on its head (or puts it back on its feet) by locating ethics in the problem of bearing witness to bare life as what founds, and at the same time ruins, any experience of subjectivity. This, then, is an ethics that does not forget or efface bare life, and so does not forget our exposure to death.

Of course, Agamben has only sketched this new ethics, and many commentators have remarked on the difficulty of drawing out the concrete implications of his work. It seems very difficult to 'apply' this ethics to situations such as that of the patient with PVS. What is important, though, is that it makes us try to think what has happened to ethics after Auschwitz and the risks of any ethics that tries to save us from our exposure to death by denying that exposure. This is a challenge that has to be faced if we are to construct an ethics of death in modern culture. Certainly, Agamben does not provide us with the reassurance of practical measures for dealing with these situations of exposure to death but he does force us to re-examine our ethics in the light of these situations. As we can see, the problem of death in modern culture is not some marginal problem but central to our culture, to our ethics, our art and our politics. Perhaps one practical implication of his work is that we must begin from the experience of shame as our new ethical material. To do this we must return to the problem of the remnant that power produces and refuse to see this as a leftover to be disposed of. If we try to dispose of the remnant, then we dispose of our humanity, and to say that mere biological existence lacks value is to risk just this danger. We should not be so confident in our judgements about lives that have value and those that do not.

CONCLUSION: ETHICS AND BARE LIFE

What we have seen is that contemporary ethics, and especially bioethics, tends to repeat the abandoning of bare life. In doing so, it repeats the gesture of power that leaves bare life as the remnant of pure survival. It does this by constructing an ethical subject that is based on the exclusion of bare life. What is ethical is whatever cannot be reduced to this state, whether that be dignity, respect, the capacity to communicate, the value of life or the capacity for truth. This means that, when ethics constructs the ethical subject, it leaves bare life in the position of inclusive exclusion: included as the basis of the ethical subject, due to the fact we are living beings, but excluded, because what makes us ethical is something else. In the case of Peter Singer's bioethics we saw how he defined his quality of life ethic by seeing the value of life defined in terms of ethically relevant capacities. These capacities are based on bare life, on our living being, but exclude mere biological existence as of no value. This is a perfect example of how an ethics of life excludes the problem of life and death that lies at the heart of our culture.

Any substantial bioethics would be an ethics that could properly think and analyse life, including life exposed to death. Badiou offered us a powerful critique of ethics, and of bioethics especially. He pointed out how it is dependent on splitting the ethical subject into those who are suffering victims and those who must rescue these victims. In Agamben's terms ethics is based around the split between bare life and political life; life exposed to death and life that can intervene on bare life. However, Badiou's own attempt to construct a new ethics and a new ethical subject is flawed. When he regards his ethics of truth as based on the capacity for truth, which excludes our animal existence, or only uses it as the basis for ethics, then he repeats the gesture of sovereign power. This is another example of the inclusive exclusion of bare life: included as bare life is the ground of our engagement with a truth process, but excluded because this bare life is put aside in finding truth. We can see here the difficulty in constructing an ethics that can respond to our exposure to death in modern culture, an ethics after Auschwitz.

The importance of Agamben's ethics is that it begins from the absolute exposure of bare life to power. What he insists on is that this problem should not be put aside or minimised in the name of ethics. Instead, ethics must deal with the shame we feel before the 'Muslim' and before our own experience of bare life. The real 'basis' of modern ethics must be that strange 'basis' bare life, which ruins our sense of subjectivity and dislocates our identity. Although his arguments are difficult, and it is difficult to translate them into practical terms, his point is actually straightforward and powerful. As he writes, 'no ethics can claim to exclude a part of humanity, no matter how unpleasant or difficult that humanity is to see' (RA: 64). This is not to imply that we must accept our exposure to death and to survival on the verge of death, but it is to insist that we cannot simply deny the situation of death in modern culture. However, ethics is not the only place where this encounter with our exposure to death has taken place. In fact, it may be that art is one of the most significant places where we have encountered death in Western culture, and where we can chart our response to the exposure to death.

NOTES

1. For a literary description of PVS that is also medically accurate, see Chuck Palahniuk's *Diary: A Novel* (2003).
2. Peter Hallward's *Badiou: a Subject to Truth* (2003) provides a detailed and clear introduction to Badiou's philosophy.
3. For a more detailed discussion of Badiou's ethic of truths and its problems, see my article 'Badiou's Fidelities: Reading the *Ethics*' (Noys, 2003).

CHAPTER 5

Transgressive Death

Neither the sun nor death can be looked at steadily.

La Rochefoucauld, *Maxims*

INTRODUCTION: THE BIRTH OF TRANSGRESSIVE DEATH

The shattering effects of sex and death obsessed the French intellectual Georges Bataille (1897–1962). His erotic novels, such as the *Story of the Eye* (1928), and his other writings constantly explore how sex and death together take us beyond the limits of our bodies, forcing us to break down in anguished laughter. In 1925 his psychoanalyst presented him with a photograph. It showed Fou-Tchou-Li, a young Chinese man, being tortured to death by the punishment of the 'hundred pieces'. The victim is tied to a post with the flesh sliced from his chest and blood streaming down his body. The executioner slices through his leg at the knee, and the upturned face of the tortured man bears a strange expression. He appears to be smiling, perhaps his face is contorted in agony or perhaps in ecstasy, or the expression may be the result of the administration of opium to prolong his torture, we do not know. At the conclusion of his last work, *The Tears of Eros* (1961), Bataille turned to this photograph, which had obsessed him throughout his life. He saw it as representing 'the identity of these perfect contraries, divine ecstasy and its opposite, extreme horror' (1989: 207). This photograph was, for Bataille, the image of ecstasy and horror.[1]

Bataille is proposing that death be thought of as transgressive: a shattering experience that overcomes us with a sense of horror and sexual pleasure. Like sex, death involves the breaking down of the boundaries of the body and both are sites of social anxiety. This concept of death as transgressive has been particularly influential on modern art. From the origins of modern art in the movements of Dada and surrealism to the contemporary Young British Artists, transgressive death is everywhere. We can find it in the repetitive images of car crashes and the electric chair in the work of the American artist Andy Warhol (1928–1987) or in the work 'Hell' (1998–2000) by contemporary British artists Jake and Dinos Chapman. This work consists of nine miniature landscapes showing over 5,000 figures, including skeletons, Nazi soldiers and human mutations, which the brothers hand-cast and painted. The scenes show concentration camps and mass graves filled with hundreds of mutilated bodies. Although artists have always represented death in modern art, this representation of death is often linked to a desire to shock and to sex. Modern art explores death, in the wake of Bataille, as a site of defilement and excess.

Transgressive death even finds its place in popular fiction. The Thomas Harris novel *Hannibal*, focused on the evil psychiatrist Hannibal Lecter, mentions that the police photographs of Hannibal Lecter's outrages are 'second in popularity only to the execution of Fou-Tchou-Li' (1999: 47) for Internet ghouls. Is this linking together of sex and death by Bataille really so modern? In his opera *Tristan and Isolde* (1865) the nineteenth-century composer Richard Wagner explored the idea of the *Liebestod* or love-death. The experience of his music tries to convey what, at first, might seem an impossible or contradictory link between love and death. If we go back further into the past, we can find the link between sex and death made relentlessly in the works of the French novelist the Marquis de Sade (1740–1814), a major influence on Bataille. Sade's novel *The 120 Days of Sodom* (1785) is an encyclopaedia of perversion in which death, like sex, is thought of as a transgression, 'which tears man from his daily life, from rational society, from his monotonous work, in order to make him undergo a paroxysm, plunging him into an irrational, violent, and beautiful world' (Ariès, 1974: 57).

However, Bataille's aesthetic of transgressive death is modern because it is the result of the new forms of exposure to death in modern culture. His aesthetic of transgressive death can be seen as focused on bare life, which becomes the central concept of his thought. Although bare life has always been with us, it takes up a central place in modern culture; in the same way, in Bataille's work, bare life takes centre stage. He transforms bare life, life on the verge of death, into a shattering erotic experience that we must confront. This accounts for his influence on modern art, which also circles around bare life. What is problematic is that Bataille tries to celebrate the exposure of life to death in modern culture. In doing so he takes us away from any understanding of bare life in political terms and turns it into something aesthetic. We are left with an art of transgressive death but this art could always simply be a 'new pornography of death' (Berridge, 2002: 243–69). In this chapter modern art and its desire for transgressive death will be analysed. This will involve returning to the work of Bataille, but also criticising it for its failure to consider how we are exposed to death in modern culture. Certainly his work is ambiguous, and this must be recognised, but his influence seems to leave us at the mercy of death. Our only option is, it seems, to revel in becoming bare life.

MODERN ART AND THE PASSION FOR THE REAL

The French philosopher Alain Badiou has argued that the key feature of the twentieth century was its passion for the real. What he meant by this is that in the twentieth century the passion was for delivering the thing itself, so, for example, not simply communism as an idea but actual communism. The nineteenth century imagined communism, the twentieth century put it into practice. To deliver the real means disrupting day-to-day 'reality', as we usually accept it, to uncover the fundamental experience that it obscures: this is the Real with a capital 'R'. We can understand the desire for transgressive death, expressed by Bataille and modern art, as another sign of this 'passion for the real'. Here the desire to deliver the real takes the form of trying to grasp death itself, in all its horror and fascination. To reach it requires an act of violent transgression, which will shatter day-to-day reality and leave the real exposed. Bataille is 'the philosopher of the passion for the Real' (Zizek, 2003: 54), and so is also the philosopher of the twentieth century. He is also the philosopher of modern art as the art of death. Modern art too has tried to deliver us death as real, especially by fracturing the limits of the body. The photographs of the tortured body of Fou-Tchou-Li show the body which modern art has been fascinated with, and the void into which transgression leads us.

Can we really reach the real? When we reach for transgressive death as the real, all we are left with is the spectacle of the real. This is true of Bataille; the only way we can approach transgressive death is through the photographs of Fou-Tchou-Li. To actually face transgressive death would be to die ourselves! It might also be that the real today increasingly takes the form of the spectacle. If we consider the attack on the World Trade Center on 11 September 2001, then this attack was not only intended to kill and destroy but also to create a spectacle of death and destruction. Those who carried out this attack wanted to produce not only material damage but also a spectacular effect as well. The Slovenian philosopher Slavoj Zizek has argued that there is an element of truth in the provocative statement by the German composer Karl-Heinz Stockhausen that the attack was 'the greatest work of art in the entire cosmos' (Zizek, 2002: 11). This statement was seen as callous toward the victims of the attack and their friends and families. However, it does draw attention to the act as a spectacle, and the images were repeated constantly on television in the wake of the attack. The exposure to the real of death is the exposure to the image of death.

A less contentious example of this effect is the Japanese horror film *The Ring* (1998) (remade in an inferior American version with the same title in 2002). The film concerns a mysterious videotape containing eerie images. If this tape is watched, then the viewer receives a phone call announcing that they will die in seven days. The only way to avoid death is to persuade someone else to watch the tape and to die in one's place. Viewing an image causes death and, of course, the whole effect is staged within a film so the distinction between real death and the image of death becomes confused. What this film demonstrates is that today the real, including death, takes the form of '*a nightmarish apparition*' (Zizek, 2002: 19). So the passion for the real and the passion for transgressive death must deal with our culture of images. We are not so much exposed to the reality of death but to the image of the reality of death, and this image may well be the reality of death today. This is the problem that confronts modern art. While it constantly tries to provide us with a direct experience of the real, through transgressive death or through bodily suffering (cosmetic surgery, scarification, blood letting, S & M, etc.), it only ever provides us with more images.

In fact, the passion for the real in modern art might be a symptom of its attempt to escape from the hold of images. Contemporary artists have often tried to produce works that present violence literally. An example is the Austrian artist Hermann Nitsch (b. 1938), founder of the group of artists known as the Viennese Actionists or direct art. In the 1960s he began staging ceremonies, what he considered to be primeval rituals, in which animals were slaughtered and the blood and remains smeared over him. He has said that 'In the fifties the most diverse artists from all over the world were confronted with the insufficiency of their respective media. They proceeded to '*Aktionen*' [actions] and happenings with real events, that may be tasted, smelt, seen, heard and touched. This was the breakthrough to reality' (in Beyst, 2002: 5). We could also say that this is the breakthrough to the real that has fascinated modern art. It is also a breakthrough to reality that challenges the limits of artistic forms and exhibition spaces. These ceremonies were designed to shatter the complacency of a conservative postwar Austria that had refused to come to terms with its Nazi past. But, again, they turn into images; even breaking out of the studio or gallery and into public space is not enough, as these ceremonies still remain spectacles.

The desire to break through to reality, the passion for the real, can be a refusal to come to terms with our culture as a culture of images. The hope is always that something lies outside the image, whether that is death, suffering or the body. What these artists actually desire is not just to shock and destroy our sense of reality but also to find the real 'reality' which is concealed by images. Although they often appear as highly transgressive, what they seek is some point of stability that would arrest the play of images and finally produce the breakthrough to reality. The paradox is that transgressive artists may not be as transgressive as they so often appear. They are probing the limits of our culture to find some basis, some reality, which has been denied to them.

Death here functions as something of a test case. It resists the image but also can only be represented through images. This is also true of transgressive death, when artists take up death for its shock value. The risk is that not only do artists never escape the problem of the image but also 'the dead are of concern only when either violating some existing prohibition or offering themselves up as images of torture' (Armitage in Virilio, 2003: 7). Of course, Bataille's celebration of the Chinese torture victim commits both these sins at the same time. Are modern artists really coming to terms with life exposed to death? When they create images of death, do they really shatter reality or simply show that today reality, including death, is dominated by images? Finally, in celebrating transgressive death, do they obscure bare life and our exposure to death?

MODERN ART AS PITILESS ART

These questions become pressing if we take a more critical stance towards modern art and its 'passion for the real' or its passion for transgressive death. The French theorist Paul Virilio has been highly critical of the effects of technology on our culture and especially the modern cult of speed. He has also extended his criticisms to contemporary art, which he regards as a pitiless art that revels in representations of pain and suffering. Instead of modern art providing us with the real, it simply reinforces our exposure to death and mimics the new deadly forces of contemporary political power. Virilio is particularly critical of avant-garde art, which he sees as the pitiless exploitation of suffering. He links this celebration of death and violence to the violence of modern totalitarian states, from the Nazis to the Cambodian Khmer Rouge regime, which slaughtered as many as 1.5 million people between 1975 and 1979. If these regimes literally kill and torture, then, in doing so, they actually realise the fantasies of those artists who only represent death and suffering. Virilio's argument is highly controversial and ignores the fact that avant-garde artists have often been critical of these regimes and have also often been persecuted by them.

The position that he takes on modern art places him in the company of the most reactionary and conservative critics of art. Despite these failings, Virilio does raise one crucial question: how do we, and how should we, represent suffering and death? He also explores how the rise of modern art as pitiless art is linked to our contemporary media culture. What modern art and the media share is an obsession with sensationalism. It is no surprise that the key term of contemporary art is 'sensation', not least in Charles Saatchi's 1997 'Sensation' exhibition of the new British art. Saatchi, once head of an advertising firm, promoted the new young British artists in terms that appealed to shock and transgression. The exhibition combined avant-garde art with the culture of British tabloid newspapers in a bizarre alliance. For Virilio, modern art and the media go hand in hand as both exploit the sensational and attack us with shock tactics. This new culture of shock uses the speed of modern media technologies to overcome our capacities for response and leaves us reeling. The result is that modern art offers no criticism of the media image but simply becomes another type of media image.

This sensational art is art that is 'in-yer-face', art that allows the viewer no space to consider, reflect or apply their 'intelligence'. In fact, one recent book on contemporary British theatre has celebrated it as 'in-yer-face theatre' (Sierz, 2001). Aleks Sierz takes up the work of young British playwrights like Sarah Kane, whose first play *Blasted* (1995) used raw language and images of rape, eye-gouging and cannibalism. The British press quickly denounced the play: *The Daily Mail* called it 'this disgusting feast of filth' and the *Sunday Telegraph* described it as a 'gratuitous welter of carnage'. Kane herself would tragically commit suicide at the age of 28 in 1999 after writing four more plays. Although Virilio does not discuss this case, it is another example of the way in which the avant-garde and the media can become linked together. In this case, it involved travestying Kane's work and focusing almost solely on the shocking content of her work while leaving her formal innovations aside.

In Virilio's diatribe, art, media, politics and culture form an almost seamless 'mediascape' of images and sound, which leave us no space or time to criticise or even think. He has a particular horror of one contemporary form of art, which for him embodies the most extreme consequences of a sensational and pitiless art. This is the new 'transgenic art' practised by artists like Stelarc and Orlan. Stelarc is an Australian cyber artist who explores the interactions between humans and technology, both computer technology and the new biotechnologies (his web site is at http://www.stelarc.va.com. au). The body artist Orlan is perhaps best known for her work where she undergoes plastic surgery to become the living embodiment of the image of women painted by the old masters (Ince, 2000). These artists take up the tools of biomedical science such as plastic surgery, drugs and prosthetic enhancements. In their passion for the real, artists have not only moved out of the studio and into the streets but into their *own bodies*, which become the work of art. For Virilio this experimentation exposes our bodies to science and encourages 'clinical voyeurism' (2003: 43).

If artists are becoming like scientists, then scientists are becoming like artists. Virilio is critical of what he calls extreme sciences that threaten 'to *break the being*, the unicity of humankind, through the impending explosion of a genetic bomb that will be to biology what the atomic bomb was to physics' (2003: 55). The taboo-breaking activity of artists paves the way for scientific work that obeys no ethical constraints and which experiments on bodies for the sake of it. We can find a warning about the consequences of this process in Alastair Reynolds's science fiction novella *Diamond Dogs* (2002). The story includes the character Dr Trintignant, described as an 'experimental cyberneticist', who is the model of the dangerous future fusion between artist and scientist. He carries out perverse experiments in body modification and the melding of flesh and machine. His work is driven as much by aesthetic concerns as it is medical or scientific, as he strives to produce the most 'beautiful' combination of man and machine. The result is the 'diamond dogs', humans modified so radically that they can no longer be considered human at all. It is this nightmare that Virilio is warning us of.

He alerts us to the risks involved with the values of experimentation and transgression in modern art. Virilio also suggests that art can exploit and violate bodies, especially bodies reduced to the state of bare life. The problem is that his warnings are often overstated and reductive: nearly all avant-garde modern art is condemned out of hand. The idea that modern art is pitiless depends on a series of value judgements that modern art has set out to question. As in the case of Hermann Nitsch, the intention of modern artists is to use such extreme images to challenge the complacency of modern Western societies, which all too often render pain and death invisible. Also, if modern art is at risk of sensationalism, is this to do with the art itself or the way in which it is taken up by the media? The example of Sarah Kane demonstrates how the media concentrate on the shocking content of modern art at the expense of any understanding of its more formal effects and without any knowledge of the history of art. These reservations suggest that we need a more complicated understanding of the fascination of modern art with transgressive death, rather than Virilio's blanket dismissal.

To do this we must pursue the issue of sensation in modern art and assess whether it can always be mistaken for sensationalism. One modern artist who has explored the problem of sensation in his work and in his reflections on his art is the twentieth-century painter Francis Bacon (1909–1992). He is renowned for his brutal images of suffering bodies, such as in his painting 'Triptych – August 1972'. This work shows three human figures each located against the background of a black doorway and each violently distorted. In particular, the central figure seems to be almost dissolving and is virtually draining out of the picture. Is this an example of pitiless art exploiting human suffering? Bacon's images are not so much about sensationalism but about the desire to convey sensation instead. To explore this I shall turn to the analysis of his work by the French philosopher Gilles Deleuze (1925–1995) in his book *Francis Bacon: the Logic of Sensation* (2003). This analysis will allow us to reflect more carefully on the representation of transgressive death in modern art.

FRANCIS BACON'S AESTHETIC OF LIFE

For Deleuze, 'what fascinates [Bacon] are the invisible forces that model flesh or shake it' (2003: x). It is the effects of these 'invisible forces' that can be seen in the painting 'Triptych – August 1972', in the fragmentation and disruption of the human form. However, these invisible forces do not simply mirror the violence of the twentieth century. According to Deleuze the violence at work in Bacon's painting is something entirely different. It is not the violence of 'spectacles of horror', although these can easily be found in Bacon's painting, but another sort of violence: 'violence that is involved only with colour and line: the violence of a sensation (and not of a representation)' (Deleuze, 2003: x). However, does this violence of sensation always collapse back into spectacles of horror, or into sensationalism?

According to Deleuze, Bacon always rejects those of his paintings that are too sensational because they tend to reduce the painting to a story. He is resisting, in advance, the kind of criticism that will be made by Virilio. Bacon is not telling a story about the violence of the twentieth century, or revelling in that violence, but instead exploring what he calls the 'violence of paint'.

The more Bacon's works are reduced to being stories about the violence of the world, of torture, of political violence or of mass death, the more the central issue of his work is dismissed. He is not aiming at representing the horrors of modern culture but at a painting that can free up the experience of sensation, which is more to do with colour and line than it is to do with suffering and death. For Virilio this kind of gesture can only be the symptom of a pitiless art that mirrors the violence of the times. Bacon is trying to break with this concept entirely. Certainly his work is violent, and certainly it has some relationship to the violence of his times, but he is not trying to render this in his work. In fact, for Deleuze, Bacon's work is not pitiless at all. On the contrary, the feeling that dominates in Bacon's painting is not horror but 'an intense pity: pity for the flesh, including the flesh of dead animals' (Deleuze, 2003: xi).

So it may be possible to have an art that shatters bodies, an art that explores the violence and pleasure of death, which is also an art of pity. The feeling of pity emerges from sensation. Where does Bacon find sensation? Deleuze suggests that one way in which Bacon finds sensation is by deconstructing the body. This act is clear if we consider Bacon's 'Study after Velázquez's Portrait of Pope Innocent X' (1953), the famous 'screaming Pope' painting. Bacon regards this painting as an attempt to paint the scream, and what we see is the image of a man being dragged upwards by the vertical strokes of the painting. Under the force of the scream the head of the Pope is pulled apart, almost 'melting', as the silent scream escapes from his mouth. One way to view this painting is as the representation of an act of violence against the body. The Pope in his chair appears like someone being executed in the electric chair or the victim of some terrible torture. This would be to supply the painting with a narrative, it would tell the story of our times as times of violence. Bacon views the painting differently, the violence of the image concerns the sensation of the scream portrayed through the lines of paint and the dissolving effects of colour, which mark the face of the Pope figure. The body is deformed and drawn out by the force of sensation.

For Deleuze, what Bacon does to the body is to transform it into a figure. The figure is the form of the painting itself or the violence of sensation, colour and line. All painting can be seen as the conflict between this figure and what Deleuze calls figuration, which is the turning of the figure into a story. In the example of the screaming Pope painting, we can turn it into a story about torture, death or the violence of power. However, this is an act of figuration that ignores the body as figure, the body collapsing or dissolving into the paint itself. The same tension can be seen in the 'Triptych – August 1972'. These images of three violated bodies could be turned into a story about the violence of modern culture: the progressive dissolving of the body and its reduction to an obscene liquid mass in the central image. What would be missed, though, would be how this dissolution of the body drags the body into the fields of colour in the painting, as can be seen in the strange pinkish 'liquid' into which the bodies are dissolving. To transform the body into a figure is to extract it from figuration, and to extract it from the usual form of the body.

If we view these images as images of sensation, this does not mean we have to abandon the feeling of pity. Virilio reads nearly all images of violence as simply reflecting the horrors of the twentieth century, as pitiless. Bacon and Deleuze argue that the painting of sensation breaks with the representation of suffering, it does not reflect the times. But this does not mean that pity disappears; instead, the dissolution of the body under the effect of the invisible forces of sensation creates the feeling of an intense pity for flesh. This, then, answers the sweeping criticisms offered by Paul Virilio. What he fails to consider is that modern art might be offering a more complex interrogation of artistic form through violence. Modern art is not simply an art obsessed with violence or with transgressive death; it is not simply an art of sensationalism. By seeing every attempt to create an image of violence or death as sensationalist, Virilio ignores the problem of sensation altogether, leaving us with a very limited understanding of modern art. He might raise important questions about the values of modern art, especially in an age in which culture has become more and more obsessed with the image, but he rules out modern art's criticism of the image. In the case of

Francis Bacon, and he is only one example of many I could have chosen, the logic of sensation is what is key. What is the result of art that focuses on this logic of sensation?

Deleuze makes a very strange argument. Despite all the violence at work in Bacon's paintings, and despite all the spectacles of horror we can find there, he suggests that actually in these works 'Abjection becomes splendor, the horror of life becomes a very pure and intense life' (Deleuze, 2003: 52). We see abjection, we see images of horror and suffering, where the body is reduced to an abject and pitiful state, to filth. The abject is the corpse, the crucified body, which fascinated Francis Bacon for many years. But, Deleuze claims, this abjection becomes splendour, and the horror of life becomes a pure and intense life. It might be that Bacon is actually offering us an aesthetics of life, and that his work is optimistic rather than pessimistic. Although I have suggested that modern art is obsessed with transgressive death, it seems that Francis Bacon is an important exception. If his work, which seems so obsessed with death, can be seen as an aesthetic of life, then this argument might well hold for many other works of modern art. However, if Bacon is offering an aesthetic of life, this still leaves the problem of bare life. Bare life is life, but life that is exposed to death. To create art which deals with the abjection and horror of the body means that this art cannot simply be an aesthetic of life that has nothing to do with death.

In fact, Bacon's celebration of intense life, like Bataille's celebration of intense death, risks obscuring the importance of bare life, and of our exposure to death, in modern culture. Of course, there is no reason why we should expect artists to engage with these questions, but the work which Bacon produced and the general fascination in modern art with transgressive death suggest that they are engaged with bare life, whether aware of it or not. Bacon's work cannot be reduced to bare life, as if bare life were the real answer to analysing his subject-matter or aesthetic. The importance of Deleuze's reading is that he makes clear how this artist and many others are reacting not only to the culture in which they live but also to the culture of art itself. What is suggestive about Deleuze's analysis of Bacon is that bare life can be approached from the position of life as well as from the position of death. It remains, as I suggested, the void around which modern art circles.

GEORGES BATAILLE'S AESTHETIC OF DEATH

Now I want to return to Georges Bataille's contrasting approach to bare life, with his celebration of intense death. It is surprising that Bataille's work has had so little impact on the field of death studies and particularly on the study of the aesthetics of death (for an exception see Dollimore, 1998: 249–57). This is particularly surprising because of his influence on contemporary thought, on modern art, and because his work is so death obsessed. Perhaps it is because his insistent linking together of death and sex still remains disturbing and even scandalous. It may also be because of the fragmentary, contradictory and complex nature of Bataille's own writings. These two problems could even be related: a thinking of sex and death together as limit-experiences can only ever lead to a writing that is fragmentary, contradictory and complex. Despite these difficulties, Bataille's attempts to explore transgressive death often have their own peculiar clarity and force; they take up a task that is, at once, existential, cultural and aesthetic.

Bataille recognises that to confront transgressive death always requires us to confront the spectacle of death. His passion for the real does not ignore the fact that the real can only appear as a nightmarish apparition. He insists that the confrontation with death always requires the detour of a spectacle – of an aesthetic, we could say. It is in Bataille's article 'The Practice of Joy Before Death', published in June 1939, that we can find his most concise articulation of this problem. Written on the verge of the Second World War and with an acute awareness of the destruction to come, it can be read as another manifesto of modern death. What Bataille finds in death is an experience where 'infinite pain turns into the joy of highest bliss' (Zizek, 2003: 54). This is the practice of joy before death and it requires us to do what La Rochefoucauld said was impossible: to look at death steadily.

To look at death steadily requires a practice of joy, but this does not mean that we escape our horror of death. Instead, as Bataille explained in one of his later essays:

If I envisage death gaily, it is not that I too say, in turning away from what is frightening: 'it is nothing' or 'it is false.' On the contrary, gaiety, connected with the work of death, causes me anguish, is accentuated by my anguish, and in return exacerbates that anguish: ultimately, gay anguish, anguished gaiety cause me, in a feverish chill, 'absolute dismemberment,' where it is my joy that finally tears me apart, but where dejection would follow joy were I not torn all the way to the end, immeasurably. (Bataille, 1990: 25)

Joy before death is not in contradiction with the anguish I also experience before death. We must meld these two states together, so that anguish leads to joy and joy back to anguish. This process must be carried to the point where I am torn apart in the face of death. It is this experience that he aims at in 'The Practice of Joy Before Death'. Bataille does not set out just to describe this experience but also to provoke it, and so to lead the reader to the point where they too can live with transgressive death.

To get to this point we must feel the force of death as an intensity that shakes us out of our everyday routine. Our day-to-day life is only 'a risk-free charade' (Bataille, 1985: 235) in which we have no real sense of death. What we must do is to feel the force of death within us, the threat of our own death, and this shatters our feeling of safety. However, once we find ourselves facing the threat of death, we can always avoid the shattering effects of this experience. One way to do this is to rush into death 'in terrified haste' (Bataille, 1985: 236). If we take this option, the path of suicide or the desire to become one with death, then we evade the truly rending effect of this encounter. Bataille is not calling for us to celebrate death through our own destruction, and he is not suggesting that we find peace in death. In his poem 'Ode to a Nightingale' (1819) the English Romantic poet John Keats (1795–1821) wrote, 'I have been half in love with easeful Death' (1996: 64). Death, for Bataille, is not easeful, and he does not agree with the Romantic desire for death: to be half in love with death is to resist the rupture of death. His work is not part of the cult of suicide or the celebration of the suicidal artist, which has dominated modern culture – from the German writer Heinrich von Kleist (1777–1811), who killed himself as part of a suicide pact, to the rock singer Kurt Cobain (1967–1994), who shot himself leaving a suicide note ending with the words 'I love you, I love you'.

Bataille said that to rush into death is to confront 'death in such a way that nothing is more horrible' (1985: 236). Instead of standing outside or inside death, we must stand before death through the practice of joy. When we stand before death, we experience the 'happy *loss of self*' as a 'kind of tragic jubilation' (Bataille, 1985: 237). Death itself would be the end of our existence and avoiding death would leave us in the illusory state of peace. Therefore the practice of joy before death might best be understood as an aesthetic of death, a new or modern art of death. This new art of death does not involve us in the preparation for a good death. It is unlike the traditional *ars moriendi*, which tried to prepare Christian believers for the afterlife. Instead, it is an art of death in which we expose ourselves to the spectacle of death in such a way that we experience an anguished joy. This is an art of death because it still requires mediation, and it still requires the spectacle or image of death if we are not to plunge too rapidly into death. What does this experience actually consist of? How might we create an aesthetic of transgressive death?

Bataille's attempts to do this are somewhat disappointing. On the one hand, he insists that 'it is impossible to give in a few pages more than the vaguest representations of that which by nature cannot be grasped' (1985: 236). The practice of joy before death shatters representation and the aesthetic. But, on the other hand, Bataille cannot resist offering descriptions of joy before death, and these descriptions are not vague at all but pathetically literal. He invokes transgressive death through the most predictable of signifiers: 'annihilation', 'this dark unknown', 'multiplied and incessant agony', 'unintelligible and bottomless space', etc. By writing about the practice of joy before death in these terms Bataille fails to carry out the task that he had announced: 'it is necessary to strip away all external representations from what is there, until it is nothing but a pure violence, an interiority, a pure inner fall into a limitless abyss' (1985: 238).

Despite the fact that these representations are intended to be shocking and transgressive, they are profoundly unshocking because they are so predictable. There is no fall into a limitless abyss but only a limited aesthetic where Bataille is reduced to imagining the frozen moment of his own death. In doing so he turns death into his own possession and his aesthetic is nothing more than that of contemporary horror fiction. The desire to pass into transgressive death leads Bataille into something of a dead end. A similar process can be found in popular fiction that plays with transgressive death.

Thomas Harris's *Hannibal* (1999) tries to portray the horrifying murders of its anti-hero Hannibal Lecter in more and more extreme ways. The novel ends with him eating the brain of a victim whom he keeps conscious throughout the procedure with surgical drugs. Although this death is meant to be terrifying, it descends into bathos. The more transgressive the novel becomes, the more it leaves behind any sense of realism and passes into the realm of horror as farce.

In his excellent introductory book on Bataille, Paul Hegarty has pointed out that Bataille's aesthetic writings 'contain both the best and the worst elements of his obsessions: on the one hand we get dynamic dispersal of form, content, subjectivity; on the other, a simplistic liking for a pseudo-gothic aesthetic' (Hegarty, 2000: 144). As we have seen, 'The Practice of Joy Before Death' is caught in just this contradiction. It tries to provide us with an aesthetic of transgressive death in which artistic form and content, and our subjectivity, are fragmented and dispersed. But instead of getting an intense death, which is the pure fall into a limitless abyss, we get the clichés of the pseudo-Gothic aesthetic. Also, it often seems that Bataille's simplistic liking for the pseudo-Gothic aesthetic is what has been most influential on contemporary art and culture. The celebration of transgressive death becomes the celebration of the most conventional ideas of what is shocking. In this case transgression is no longer breaking limits but instead is limited to what we find shocking (Noys, 1998). How are we to account for Bataille's failure to construct an aesthetic of death?

AGAMBEN'S CRITICISMS OF BATAILLE

Agamben explains this impasse as the result of Bataille's attempt to celebrate bare life as the experience of transgressive death. When Bataille celebrates bare life, he does not grasp the actual situation of bare life. He does not see the production of bare life as an act of power but, instead, tries to turn it into transgressive death. His aesthetic can only ever be disappointing because it evades the fundamental problem. The same point could also be made in relation to Deleuze trying to see Francis Bacon's work as an aesthetic of life. Although this reading surprises us, it seems weak when we actually consider

Bacon's paintings. His paintings might be better understood as another confrontation with bare life, this time from the position of life rather than of death. But, in different ways, the aesthetic of intense death and the aesthetic of intense life avoid properly confronting bare life, although they depend upon it. The case of Bataille can demonstrate how this happens. What, precisely, is Bataille's mistake?

For Agamben he makes two mistakes: first he tries to separate out and celebrate bare life; secondly, in doing so, he obscures the political issue of power that bare life poses. The importance of Bataille's thinking is that he does raise the question of bare life, even if he mistakes its nature. Bataille must be credited with having 'proposed the radical experience of this bare life' (HS: 112) but when he links together sex with death he obscures this radical experience. In separating out and pinning down the experience of bare life, whether in the photographs of the Chinese torture victim or in the practice of joy before death, he unwittingly performs the same operation as sovereign power. As we have seen, sovereign power works by dividing off bare life to make it available to being dominated. Like Foucault, Bataille cannot see the link between sovereign power and bare life. In fact, he compounds his error by trying to turn the experience of bare life into the experience of sovereignty. Bataille's concept of sovereignty is very different to Agamben's. For Bataille it means the experience of exposure to death and the ability to practise joy before death, but this means missing completely the political nature of sovereign power. When we try to find bare life and sovereignty together, in the extreme experience of transgressive death, we do not consider the link between bare life and sovereign power, and the result is catastrophic.

It is catastrophic because the political decision on death is obscured, and this is Bataille's second mistake. The body of the sacred man is not the body of transgressive death but a political body. When we face the photographs of the Chinese torture victim, we are not confronted with the strange experience of transgressive death but with a body exposed to power. The fact that this body is reduced to an abject state where it can be killed but is not sacrificed is not to be celebrated. Instead this 'contradiction' must be explained politically as the result of the abandonment of bare life. Bataille's pseudo-Gothic aesthetic is not only puerile but also dangerous. What it cannot grasp is 'the violence at issue in modern biopolitics' (HS: 113). This violence is not spectacular in the sense that Bataille gives it: the public and terrible ritual of the execution. Instead the violence of modern biopolitics finds its form in places like the concentration camps: where death is confined to a particular space but allowed free reign. Bataille is trying to restore a dignity to death through making it the most abject spectacle, whereas death in modern culture finds its true horror in its very banality.

This difficulty is not answered by an aesthetic of intense life either. Again, abjection is turned to splendour, this time in the name of life rather than in the name of death. Bare life is separated off, only this time to be celebrated as life rather than as death. But whether we choose life or life exposed to death we still forget the ground of power that produces separate bare life. There is actually very little to choose between Bataille and Deleuze. Any aesthetics of transgressive death, or any aesthetics of intense life, cannot think about bare life as the production of sovereign power. It may well be that, although Virilio's warnings were shrill and excessive, they do point to something which is easily forgotten: the political context of modern art, in which the media, medicine and art all value experimentation on the body. We must interrogate our 'clinical voyeurism' before art in which the body is exposed to fragmentation and destruction.

Agamben does not discuss the issue of aesthetics in *Homo Sacer*, and this is surprising. Although his book is devoted to exploring the exposure of bodies to power, it does not deal with the exposure of bodies as images. Neither does it discuss the dominance of the modern media in contemporary society in any detail. Agamben is perfectly aware that we live in a society of images, in the society of the spectacle, but he does not discuss how images affect our exposure as bare life. In this sense his work does not deal with the problem that Jean Baudrillard posed: what is our relation to death in a culture where even death has become simulated? This leaves a large absence in his work, especially as death studies has often drawn attention to the importance of the aesthetic as a site where we try to deal with death (Dollimore, 1998). I have tried to correct this absence, while retaining Agamben's critical point about the nature of death as political, especially in modern culture. To go further than Agamben does, in order to explore the possibility of an aesthetic that would try to come to terms with bare life, require that we return to the issue of the banality of death in modern culture.

THE BANALITY OF MODERN DEATH: THE CAR-CRASH

In modern culture, Agamben states, we find 'a life that as such is exposed to violence without precedent precisely in the most profane and banal ways' (HS: 114). The celebration of transgressive death or intense life in extreme spectacles of suffering bodies actually abandons bare life. In different ways they try to give a prestige to bare life aesthetically, a prestige that it definitively lacks. How could we construct an aesthetic of bare life that is exposed to violence in the most profane and banal ways? Agamben's example of this exposure to death is the fact that 'Our age is the one in which a holiday weekend produces more victims on Europe's highways than a war campaign' (HS: 114). What he does not discuss is the art that has tried to examine this 'car-crash culture' (Brottman, 2001), in which death is random, profane and banal.

One example of car-crash art is the novel *Crash* (1975) by the British writer J. G. Ballard (b. 1930). Although Ballard is often regarded as a science fiction writer, a label that he does not reject, his work explores the limits of the effects of modern technology on the human body and psyche. In *Crash* he uses a distanced clinical prose, modelled on scientific reports, to anatomise our obsession with the car crash and its erotic dimensions. The book explores our fascination with the celebrity car crash, such as the death of the 1950s film star Jayne Mansfield at the age of 33 in 1967. Her death car, a Buick Electra 225, was actually displayed in 'Tragedy In US History Museum' before it closed in 1998. Ballard's novel has proven eerily prescient in the light of the death of Princess Diana in a car crash in August 1997, and the resulting mass mourning. Today, the Internet even includes sites devoted to the deaths of famous people in car crashes (http://www.who2. com/deathbycarcrash.html), confirming Ballard's diagnosis.

However, it could easily be argued that what Ballard gives us is another example of transgressive death that celebrates the exposure of bare life and lifts it from banality into the erotic. The novel is concerned with the perversity of the car crash, and Ballard claimed that he has written the first pornographic novel based on technology. The French theorist Jean Baudrillard has accused Ballard of missing the banality of modern death by trying to place the car crash within a new logic of perversion. In doing so, Ballard restores meaning to an event that has no meaning. Baudrillard argues that we can read the novel against this logic of perversion and find a world 'denuded of meaning' where the novel forms 'the simple mirror of torn-up bodies' (Baudrillard, 1994: 113). In Ballard's austere and blank prose we can find death that is robbed of meaning. The novel *Crash* not only celebrates death in a logic of perversion but it also exposes us to the fate of torn-up bodies that carry no sexual charge. Baudrillard finds in Ballard's novel an art of modern death that is the art of our exposure to the banality of death inflicted through modern technology. While Ballard tries to force technology to make a perverse sense, what he reveals, despite himself, is that there is no sense or meaning except the profane banality of death.

Ballard's novel indicates the difficulty in approaching the banality of modern death, and the constant temptation to transform death into something erotic and transgressive. Baudrillard's criticisms of *Crash* are a warning about the dangers of using sex to give a prestige to death that it has lost. Although Ballard tries to probe our exposure to the profane and banal car-crash death, he often remains within the same nostalgia that we have seen in Bataille. This is the nostalgia for death that has a meaning, even if that meaning is perverse. However, as Baudrillard points out, the coldly distant prose and ironic stance that Ballard takes in *Crash* puts a limit on his search for a new logic of perversion. His writing shows us that the car crash resists being seen as perverse and that it exposes us to a new form of death that is more random, unpredictable and resistant to meaning. It is in these features that we could find an aesthetic of bare life, as an aesthetic of exposure to death. This aesthetic does not celebrate intense life or intense death, it does not celebrate bare life, but instead it is an aesthetic of the banal and profane death.

David Cronenberg's 1996 film adaptation of *Crash* was widely condemned on its release for its perversity, and was described by the *London Evening Standard* as 'beyond the bounds of depravity'. However, despite its many representations of sexual transgression the film actually more closely approaches a banal 'coldness' than does Ballard's novel. The psychoanalytic critic Parveen Adams (2003) has made a powerful analysis of the film that confirms the banality of death. She stresses that, despite the fact that the film is full of bodies engaged in multiple and 'perverse' sexual acts, these bodies are represented as empty. They are not engaging sexual bodies but bodies reduced to being void, something like what we have been examining as bare life. Also, she argues that the images the film offers us are without any real depth. The 'world' that this film creates is a flattened world which lacks the sense of space we expect from the film image, and the result is the viewer is left disoriented (Adams, 2003: 162). How does it do this?

When the images of the film flatten space, they leave us without a space in which we can place ourselves in relation to this image. Film images typically create a sense of depth through creating a three-dimensional space on a two-dimensional surface. Then we, as spectators, can imagine or insert ourselves as viewers into this space. *Crash* is a film of surfaces that works by not allowing us this space. If we are deprived of our position as spectators, then we can no longer stand securely observing the film but become caught up on its surface. Although Adams does not mention Baudrillard, we could recall his comment that Ballard's novel offers us 'the simple mirror of torn-up bodies'. In the same way the film *Crash* offers us the simple mirror of these damaged bodies, depriving us of the illusion of space. As a medium working with images, the film can take this effect further and leave us with only the screen as screen.

At this point we face a claustrophobic viewing experience, as if we were thrust up against the screen or the screen thrust up against us. For Adams, this effect collapses the usual psychic space we inhabit as spectators. This effect also allows us to think of a new approach to the art of modern death. This intrusion into our space and the violent voiding of bodies in the film are both suggestive of what a new aesthetic of bare life might look like. In voiding the body we are left with a body that cannot be celebrated as an example of transgressive death. The voided body is not a perverse body or an ecstatic body, but the body of bare life as such. Also, in collapsing the space of the spectator, the film thrusts us into an encounter with that body which we cannot escape. If bare life is what lies closest to us, within us even, but which is usually excluded, then the film *Crash* suggests an aesthetic that refuses to exclude bare life. It puts us face to face with the shame that bare life provokes and forces us to witness bare life. This is an art of exposure to our exposure to death, which allows us no escape.

What we are exposed to is death as profane and banal. In this way an aesthetic of bare life must avoid the value of cherished value of 'intensity', which dominates much of contemporary art and criticism. The constant search for or celebration of intense experiences threatens to obscure the actual existence of modern death as something more banal, something that is not intense at all. Instead of celebrating intensity, celebrating transgressive death or transgressive life, we need to try to find the new aesthetic of bare life. No doubt *Crash* is not the only example of this aesthetic, and also we could return to the history of contemporary art with these new criteria in mind. What it does offer us, however, is one example that can interrogate and criticise our fascination with death as an extreme state. It also offers us the possibility of passing beyond this fascination and into the space where we are exposed to death through an aesthetic that does not try to place a meaning on death.

CONCLUSION: THE AESTHETICS OF BARE LIFE

In this chapter we have traced the path from Bataille's 'invention' of a new modern aesthetic of transgressive death to the possibility of an aesthetic of bare life. Bataille's aesthetic of transgressive death was founded on bare life, but celebrated life exposed to death as a sexual experience that could shatter our everyday existence. This idea has proved profoundly influential on modern art, which has followed his path of transgression. I have suggested that we understand this influence in terms of modern art's passion for the real, a characteristic that it shares with twentieth-century culture and politics. The passion for delivering the 'Real', with a capital 'R', is the passion for delivering the thing itself beyond normal reality. However, this passion for the real has had to negotiate the problem that modern culture is a culture of images, of what Jean Baudrillard called 'simulation'. Today the real experience of death is often the experience of the image of death, and the search for the real becomes a search amongst images. The exposure to death is often only the exposure to death on the television screen, but this is the form of the real in modern culture: the image as nightmarish apparition.

Paul Virilio has condemned this passion for the real and the focus of modern art on suffering and death as pitiless. He suggests that modern art simply mirrors the violence of modern culture, rather than criticising it.

More and more, modern art is in an unholy alliance with modern media, advertising and politics, which encourage the production of images that overwhelm our capacities for response. This is 'in-yer-face' art that sets out to shock and to turn sensation into sensationalism. The work of Francis Bacon suggested a more complicated understanding of the aims of modern art. His work tries to detach itself from sensationalism to explore the logic of sensation at work in paint itself. The 'violence of paint', Bacon suggests, is not simply the mirror of the violence of the age. According to Gilles Deleuze, Bacon's paintings actually offer us an aesthetic of intense life that cannot be mistaken for the celebration of suffering or death. Whether it is a matter of intense death or intense life, the problem of bare life still remains.

As Bataille's attempts to found an aesthetic of transgressive death demonstrate, any such intense aesthetic always risks missing the problem of bare life. Although he sets out to strip away all external representations from death, which might well be a way of finding bare life, he actually loads on to death new representations. These new representations are often the most predictable signifiers of horror and shock, and so are not very shocking! In fact, they avoid the problem of death in modern culture, where we are exposed to death outside the law and the religious. The aim of modern art has often been to display death with a 'visceral realism – death shown stripped of any coherent moral or religious reference' (Berridge, 2002: 246). What Bataille demonstrates is the difficulty of that task. His work may be founded on bare life but in his celebration of bare life it seems that Bataille wants to restore to bare life a strange new type of religious meaning.

The religious meaning he places on death is not the traditional Christian meaning, where suffering and death are redeemed in the afterlife. But Bataille's celebration of transgressive death still makes it a place where we can recover our true values in the contemplation of pain and suffering. While Bataille and other modern artists may have tried to strip death of any coherent moral or religious reference, they still often try to give death meaning. The meaning they place on death is that it can shatter the complacency of our existence and the complacency of our culture. Even when treated as meaningless, they still give death a meaning. This meaning is found by linking together sex and death as limit-experiences, which challenge the limits of our culture; the result is often a 'new pornography of death'. Rather than condemning this as immoral, I have tried to demonstrate that it is a failure to really come to terms with our exposure to death in modern culture. It is a failure to come to terms with the widespread exposure of bare life as life on the verge of death. Despite the claims that it confronts death, it may be that modern art avoids the problem of modern death.

There are signs that the art of transgressive death is becoming exhausted. This exhaustion does not mean that we must return to more 'proper' and 'appropriate' artistic subjects, and put an end to experimentation and return to order. Instead, it may give us new ways to approach the problem of our exposure to death. This is what I have called the aesthetic of bare life. I have briefly sketched how some modern art works have tried to represent death as profane and banal. The art of the car crash is only one example of the possibility of representing bare life. Again, this art is often caught in the paradox of celebrating bare life, and of remaining with the aesthetic of transgressive death. At other points, though, it does allow us to ask the question of how we are to represent our exposure to death in modern culture without simply celebrating this exposure. For Agamben, as we shall see in the next chapter, the problem of bare life is political and can only be dealt with politically. This view is limited and, as the case of modern art demonstrates when it offers an aesthetic of bare life, it challenges us to grasp our exposure to death in modern culture.

NOTES

I. Bataille's use of China as the site of transgressive death could easily be seen as another example of Western 'Orientalism' (Said, 1995) – when the Western gaze constructs the East as Other.

CHAPTER 6

Resisting Death

The absolutely desperate current state of affairs fills me with hope.

Karl Marx, Letter to Ruge, May 1843

INTRODUCTION: INCARCERATION WITHOUT END

In the new millennium we have witnessed the emergence of new spaces of power, which are also spaces of our exposure to death. These new political spaces include Camp Delta in Guantánamo Bay, Cuba, where the USA holds more than 600 prisoners. The prisoners are being held captive as part of the new global 'war against terrorism', and the Americans have classified them as 'unlawful combatants'. This means that they have been excluded from the Geneva Conventions and international human rights law. They are new figures of bare life, left utterly abandoned by the law and utterly exposed to the threat of torture or death. Although the signs are now that these prisoners will either be tried or freed, their legal situation means that they could have been left incarcerated without any prospect of release. If they are tried by the United States before military tribunals, then they will still be deprived of many basic legal rights, and these trials are highly legally dubious. Camp Delta is only one example of the bare power being exercised by states in contemporary culture. The new powers associated with the 'war against terrorism' have eroded democratic rights and seem to confirm Agamben's insights into the importance of bare life for political power.

This is further evidence that bare life did not disappear with the Nazi concentration camps, but instead that it is still the dominant factor in contemporary politics. The question that we are faced with is how we might resist the continuing extension of political power over our bodies and the exposure of our bodies to the threat of death. If this exposure is political, then this would seem to indicate that our resistance to this exposure must also be political. Agamben argues, agreeing with Marx, that the desperate state of contemporary affairs should fill us with hope. What we must hope for is the possibility of inventing a new politics that will allow us to resist our being reduced to bare life and to the state of pure survival. As we have seen, Agamben regards the attempts to save bare life through ethics and through art as extremely problematic, although he does suggest a new ethics. That new ethics is part of a wider project, and Agamben puts his hope in a new politics. This new politics is not only a matter for the lone political theorist but also a practical matter for all of us. As we are all exposed as bare life, then we all share the danger of exposure to death; at the same time, we must also all try to construct our resistance to this danger.

To analyse the possibilities for resisting our exposure to death, the comparison between Agamben's work and that of the French theorist Michel Foucault needs to be made again. In Chapter Two we saw how close Agamben was to Foucault, and how he had been inspired by his work on biopolitics. We also saw how Agamben disagreed with Foucault on the nature of power. Whereas Foucault sees modern power taking more mobile and plural forms, Agamben argued that we still live with sovereign power as the old power of death. This sovereign power has become more dispersed in modern culture, and less visible, but no less threatening. Foucault was not only one of the major thinkers of power in modern culture, he was the thinker of the resistance to power as well. For Foucault, power was always bound up with resistance, and one could not be thought without other. Agamben not only has a different understanding of power, he also has a different understanding of resistance. By comparing his work with that of Michel Foucault, we shall be able to understand what is at stake with the politics of death in modern culture and how we might resist our exposure to death.

Foucault is one of the contemporary thinkers who has done most to develop the concept of resistance to power. He always stresses that power and resistance provoke each other, and together form strange spirals. We might think of this relationship in terms of the Möbius strip, which is formed by taking a strip of paper, making a half twist in it and joining the ends together. When we trace along the Möbius strip we find that we pass from one 'side' of the strip to the other. In the same way, when we trace along relationships of power we find ourselves in relationships of resistance, and vice versa. As we shall see, Foucault links the spiralling relationship between resistance and power to both the body and life. If biopolitics is politics exercised over life (*bio*), then any resistance to biopolitics will also be a resistance of life against power. The French philosopher Gilles Deleuze has developed Foucault's argument; he was, at one time, a friend of Foucault's and he shares many of Foucault's concerns.[1] Together they have produced an influential model of political resistance based on the body and on life.

Agamben, however, is critical of the path taken by Foucault and Deleuze. He argues that, although their thinking of resistance is profoundly important, they have not understood the problem of bare life. This means that we must go beyond Foucault and Deleuze if we are to find an adequate politics to deal with our exposure to death in modern culture. For Agamben, we must find a new figure of bare life from which we can construct a new politics of resistance. He finds this figure in an unlikely place: with the refugee. The official definition of the refugee, according to the 1951 Geneva Convention (Article IA(2)), is a person who:

> owing to well founded fear of being persecuted for reasons of race, religion, nationality, membership of a particular social group or political opinion, is outside the country of his [/her] nationality and is unable or, owing to such fear, is unwilling to avail himself [/herself] of the protection of his [/her] country; or who, not having a nationality and being outside the country of his [/her] former habitual residence as a result of such events, is unable or, owing to such fear, is unwilling to return to it.

Why should the refugee be the site of a new politics? Isn't the refugee, persecuted, without protection, lacking nationality, one of the most vulnerable of people? The terrible suffering of many refugees might suggest that Agamben is detached from reality if he hopes to find any politics of resistance with this figure.

However, it is this deprivation of political identity and the fact that the refugee is stripped of his or her legal attributes which make the refugee a critical figure. Although the refugee is subject to power by being abandoned by it, Agamben also sees in this 'position' the possibility of building a new politics in exodus from power. Perhaps, he suggests, we should not simply resist sovereign power but actively flee from it, and so flee from this power of death. It is this argument that needs to be fleshed out to understand what Agamben might mean by a politics of the refugee. This politics will also be a politics that flees from our exposure to death and so the refugee might also be a crucial figure in relation to modern death. Therefore, although this chapter might seem to be exploring questions that lie outside modern death, of bodies, life, resistance and politics, we should remember that these are also all places of our exposure to death. We must take a necessary detour through these questions before we can construct a politics of modern death.

RESISTANCE AND POWER

Foucault develops a new concept of resistance in Volume I of *The History of Sexuality* writing that 'Where there is power, there is resistance, and yet, or rather consequently, this resistance is never in a position of exteriority in relation to power' (Foucault, 1979a: 95). What this means is that power and resistance are always in a relationship to each other. Resistance does not exist as some pure point outside the effects of power, and power can only ever exist in relationship to resistance. We cannot have one without the other and there is always a continuous battle being waged between forces of power and forces of resistance. Foucault also emphasises that both resistance and power consist of multiple points; as we saw in Chapter Two, there is no one centre of power for him and, also, there is no one centre of resistance. Rather than being interested in grand moments of resistance, such as revolutions, Foucault describes a whole range of micro-resistances that lack any centre or organising principle. If power is fluid, then resistance too is better thought about as made up of 'mobile and transitory points' (Foucault, 1979a: 96) that swarm through the social body.

Does this argument that power and resistance are always related to each other lead to pessimism? Is Foucault arguing that we can never get outside power and that resistance is always trapped by power? Many of his more traditional left-wing critics have thought so. One example is Edward Said (1935–2003), a leading literary critic and the pioneer of the critical analysis of imperialism and colonialism. He said that in Foucault's books there is never any doubt 'that power is going to win out in the end' and 'that the whole idea of resistance is essentially defeated from the start' (Said, 2002: 9). Also, Foucault refuses to supply any real detail about what resistance is. He leaves this category empty and many critics have objected to Foucault's failure to describe what resistance consists of. However, it can be argued that these criticisms miss the point. If power is bound up with resistance, then we could equally well say that resistance could always win in the end. In fact, Foucault is trying to get away from the idea of any final victory of either power or resistance, and he insists that we are faced with an endless struggle between them. Also, if he leaves the category of resistance empty, then this is because he does not see his role as explaining what resistance is. Resistance is not a matter for the theorist but a practical matter of what those resisting actually do.

This changes the role of the intellectual as well. His or her role is no longer to provide guidance or instruction on how we should resist. The role of the intellectual is not to be the moral conscience of the age. Foucault is critical of the 'universal intellectual' who tries to express the truth for all. Instead, he argues for a new 'specific intellectual' who will take up specific strategic issues and try to form a relay of resistance in particular struggles. Foucault himself tried to follow this model. His historical study of power and the prison, *Discipline and Punish*, was undertaken alongside his involvement with the struggles of prisoners to have their voices heard and to resist penal power. In this way the theoretical study of power was designed and written in relation to strategies of resistance practised by prisoners themselves. Foucault did not aim to speak for them but to aid them by explaining the nature of power in contemporary society and so to encourage new, inventive practices of resistance that would disturb power. His role was not to dictate or instruct people on how to resist, but to make links between practices of resistance and his new understanding of power.

All these changes to the nature of resistance are, like the changes Foucault explored in relation to power, the result of the birth of biopolitics. When politics took up the body and life as its central focus, then resistance to power would also involve bodies and life as well. The plurality of power is the result of power taking as its object the plurality of bodies and lives. If power shifts on to the terrain of the body and life, then so too must resistance. As Gilles Deleuze said, 'when power ... takes life as its aim or object, then resistance to power already puts itself on the side of life, and life turns against power' (Deleuze, 1988: 92). If we want to find resistance, then we must find it, as Deleuze and Foucault suggest, in the body and in life. Before going on to explore how they do this, we have to be aware of the problem of the category of resistance they both use. Resistance may well not just be a matter of life and bodies but also of resistance to bodies and life exposed to death.

This is what Agamben points out when he writes that 'The concept of resistance here must be understood not merely as a political metaphor but as an echo of Bichat's definition of life as "the set of functions that resist death"' (P: 232). Resistance is not only a political matter, but also a matter of life and its resistance to death. So far, this seems to be in agreement with what Foucault and Deleuze are arguing. However, Agamben goes on to ask of resistance whether it 'truly suffices to master the ambivalence of today's biopolitical conflict, in which the freedom and happiness of human beings is played out on the very terrain – bare life – that marks their subjection to power' (P: 232). What he is suggesting is that resistance forgets the problem of bare life, and forgets that the struggle over bare life is not only a matter of resistance and life but also a matter of our exposure to death. His warning stresses the limited understanding both Foucault and Deleuze have of resistance and life, when we take into account our exposure to death, our becoming bare life. This must be borne in mind as we examine how they try to find resistance in bodies and in life.

RESISTANCE AND THE BODY

Foucault does not leave the concept of resistance as empty as his critics have often claimed. Instead, at the end of Volume I of *The History of Sexuality*, Foucault mentions 'a different economy of bodies and pleasures' (1979a: 159) that might allow us to leave behind the monotony of 'that austere monarchy of sex' (1979a: 159). As the 'austere monarchy of sex' is also a monarchy of power, then Foucault is suggesting that resistance can be found in a new relationship between bodies and pleasures. This new relationship can form a 'rallying point for the counterattack against the deployment of sexuality' (Foucault, 1979a: 157), and so against power. What sort of body can resist power? This new body of resistance is not some 'pure' natural body that somehow lies outside the field of power. As we have seen, power and resistance always exist together. The body that can resist power is the body as a set of resistances that is provoked by power and which provokes power.

What is this body of resistance then? Foucault suggests that it might be possible to escape the reign of power that functions through sexuality by resisting the drive to find our truth in our sex. Instead of conceiving bodies as sexual and our sexuality as our truth, something to be confessed to or endlessly analysed, we might instead construct new practices of bodies and pleasures. These new bodies would not be bound up within the limits of sex. The relationship between bodies and pleasures would be concerned with 'fabricating other forms of pleasure, of relationships, of coexistence, attachments, loves, intensities' (Foucault, 1989b: 144). Foucault's search for this new body leads him to an interest in S & M as a new art of sexual practice, an intensification of the relationship between the body and pleasure that even takes every part of the body as a sexual instrument (Foucault, 1989b: 226). Agamben, though, is sceptical whether this new body can really be the basis for a new politics of resistance. He is wary about the claim that some new body could resolve all the problems of bare life and of our exposure to death.

This warning is important because Foucault is only one of a number of contemporary theorists who have tried to find some sort of new body that would deal with the problems of political power and offer a point of resistance. Another example is that of the American feminist theorist Donna Haraway (b. 1944) and her 'Cyborg Manifesto' (1999). In that work Haraway sees the cyborg, a being which combines machine and human being, as a way of rupturing Western dualisms. The cyborg is also the promise of a new hybrid and constructed political identity that can escape and resist power, due to the impossibility of strictly defining and containing it. Agamben would also be sceptical whether this hybrid technical body could actually solve the problem of bare life. In Chapter Five, we discussed how technological experimentation on the model could increase the domain of power over life, rather than being liberating. Although Haraway's work engages with the problems of science and biopolitics, her utopian vision of the cyborg may not break adequately with our exposure as bare life.

These new bodies cannot actually resolve the problem of bare life, and often avoid it completely. When they promise us a new body, they tend to ignore how our bodies are constructed now. In particular these new bodies avoid dealing with the contemporary situation in which our bodies are exposed to a biopolitics that has become deadly, or thanatopolitical. One of the most audacious attempts to find a new body of resistance has been undertaken by Gilles Deleuze, along with his colleague Félix Guattari (1930–1992). They have proposed the concept of the 'body without organs', which they have borrowed from the French surrealist Antonin Artaud (1896–1948). This visionary poet and playwright once wrote in a poem 'The body is the body / it stands alone / it has no need of organs / the body is never an organism / organisms are the enemies of bodies' (in Deleuze, 2003: 44); this is the 'body without organs'. Deleuze and Guattari try to develop this concept as a concept of resistance. In their joint work *A Thousand Plateaus* (1988), they ask 'How do you make yourself a body without organs?' (1988: 149–66). Their task is not to define the body without organs but instead to show that it is a kind of practice, an act or an art of the body.

This acting on the body, this art of the body, is fraught with risks. Deleuze and Guattari recognise that experiments that set out to 'deconstruct' or subvert the body can always lead to disaster: the destruction of the body. Modern culture is littered with examples of failed attempts to make ourselves a body without organs: the numbed body of the drug addict or alcoholic, the empty and frozen body of the catatonic schizophrenic, or the body of the masochist that remains trapped within one perverse scenario. Therefore, when we set out to make ourselves a body without organs, we must act with some care. The body must not simply be destroyed or shattered but acted upon so as to produce new forces and new possibilities. These experiments are also not solely individual but involve connections with other bodies. They are as much collective as they are individual. It is surprising that Deleuze and Guattari provide so few 'positive' examples of successful bodies without organs. However, this could be because, like Foucault, they wish to encourage experimentation rather than laying down plans or rules for how we should make such bodies. Their more positive examples are usually drawn from the work of artists and writers who use their art to practise an art of the body.

One of the places in which Deleuze has found this 'body without organs' is in the deconstructed bodies of Francis Bacon's paintings, discussed in the previous chapter. What we see in those paintings is the body in flux or dissolving, or bodies that seem to lack boundaries and limits. The body in these paintings becomes the body of an intense life, which is found by deconstructing the body. This act of deconstruction can appear to be destructive, but it is not a simple act of cruelty. Bacon's 'cruelty' to bodies is actually about releasing the forces of the body, releasing sensation, and not just about destroying the body (Deleuze, 2003: 45). This, for Deleuze, is the body without organs; a body that goes beyond the limits of the normal structures of the organism. It is the body as the powers of resistance, as life, that cannot be contained within the limits of the 'normal' body.

Agamben is far more critical about the idea that any such new body could promise the site for a new politics. For him, 'The "body" is always already a biopolitical body and bare life, and nothing in it, or the economy of its pleasure seems to allow us to find solid ground on which to oppose the demands of sovereign power' (HS: 187). If we talk about the 'cyborg body' or the 'body without organs', then we are really talking about a biopolitical body and bare life, a body exposed to death by power. To ignore this fact is to fail to find any real resistance to power and any real resistance to the politics of death in modern culture. The body is not 'solid ground' because the body is always decomposed by power into bare life. This means that we do not need to deconstruct the body or turn it into a hybrid body. Instead, we need to find some way out of the play of sovereign power that only leaves us as bare life, and that forces that bare life into a series of social or legal identities. If the body is not the answer, then what about life as the site of resistance?

RESISTANCE AND LIFE

For Foucault and Deleuze, when power takes life as its object, then life becomes the possibility of resistance. This is not simply the defence of the individual life, or of the 'right to life'. Instead, what Foucault and Deleuze especially find in life is a set of forces that goes beyond the individual. Life as resistance is life that exceeds the idea of identity; it refers to forces of life that are 'larger, more active, more affirmative and richer in possibilities' (Deleuze, 1988: 92). Where can we find this experience of life? Deleuze gives the most detailed description of life as resistance in his final published work, 'Immanence: A Life…' (1997). This text is particularly complex but in it he suggests that 'life' has to be understood as a kind of power or force. Life refers to nothing outside itself, it is immanent, and what it finds in itself is the power of resistance that exceeds power and exceeds identity.

This can be most easily understood if we turn to the examples of 'a life' that Deleuze examines. These examples are interesting because they raise again the question of our exposure to death. It seems that Deleuze cannot think of 'a life' without thinking of it as exposed to death, and this might well be a symptom of our exposure to death in modern culture. His first example is taken from the novel *Our Mutual Friend* (1997 [1865]) by the Victorian writer Charles Dickens (1812–1870). He finds 'a life' in the experience of one of the characters, Rogue Riderhood, who is, as his name suggests a good-for-nothing, the villain of the book. At one point in the novel this character is left in a coma, and despite the fact that he is such a rogue he attracts the sympathy of those gathered around his comatose body. As Dickens writes, 'Neither Riderhood in this world, nor Riderhood in the other, could draw tears from them; but a striving human soul between the two can do it easily' (1997: 440). What attracts their sympathy is that 'the spark of life within him is curiously separable from himself now, and they have a deep interest in it, probably because it *is* life, and they are living and must die' (Dickens, 1997: 439).

The 'spark of life' is what Deleuze calls 'a life' or life as resistance. It only emerges at the moment between life and death, when life plays with death. The moment that Rogue Riderhood starts to recover from his coma it disappears, and so does the sympathy of those around him: 'As he grows warm, the doctor and the four men cool. As his lineaments soften with life, their faces and their hearts harden to him' (Dickens, 1997: 441). The more that he recovers, the more he returns to his former, disreputable, self and the more his attendants want to be rid of him. 'A life' is then only one brief moment that appears between life and death, in exactly the situation of bare life that we examined in Chapter Three. While Deleuze is trying to find life as resistance he seems to be led back to bare life, which is life subject to power. It is almost as if Deleuze cannot escape the problem of bare life despite his best efforts to find a body or a life that will allow him to find a site of resistance. This difficulty illustrates a wider problem of trying to resist power and of trying to resist our exposure to death. To escape is not as easy as it seems to be.

Deleuze's other example is equally problematic. He now finds 'a life' in the existence of the very young child. The very young child lacks a sense of identity or individuality, but also seems to contain huge possibilities and vigour. The child is 'a life' as a set of forces that exist before these forces have become limited and confined within a particular identity. However, Deleuze has to recognise that, although the child contains these forces of power, of possibility, they are also weak and suffer. The child may not be directly exposed to death, as Rogue Riderhood was, but they are still highly vulnerable. Deleuze might have removed 'a life' from the direct moment when death is confronted but that doesn't mean that death is not still there as an indirect threat. Infancy, along with old age, is one of the most vulnerable periods of human life and, outside Western countries, infant mortality rates remain staggeringly high. According to UNICEF statistics, infant mortality for the least developed countries was 157 per 1,000 live births; for the industrialised countries it was 7 per 1,000 live births (http://www.childinfo.org/cmr/revis/db2.htm).

Although Deleuze sets out to find 'a life' that is resistance, he seems to end on the terrain of bare life. As Agamben writes, Deleuze is led 'into an area that is even more uncertain, in which the child and the dying man present us with the enigmatic cipher of bare biological life as such' (P: 230). What he cannot see is that, like the body, life is also the product of power. Does this mean that there is no escape from power? If Foucault was accused of pessimism, then isn't Agamben even more pessimistic? It certainly seems that there is no way for us to resist our exposure to death in modern culture. As Slavoj Zizek has noted, in Agamben's work 'the topics of human rights, democracy, rule of law, and so on, are ultimately reduced to a deceptive mask for the disciplinary mechanisms of "biopower" whose ultimate expression is the twentieth-century concentration camps' (Zizek, 2002: 95). He would take his place alongside other pessimistic interpretations of modern culture, which see power everywhere and no escape from its clutches.

However, despite the care and time that Agamben devotes to analysing the mechanisms and mystifications of power, he is not ruling out any political change. What we have to do though is overturn the biopolitical ground on which we find ourselves, so that we are no longer nothing but bare life. This overturning does not mean that we must abandon bare life to find some new body outside or resistant to power. If we abandon bare life, then we repeat the gesture of sovereign power that leaves bare life exposed to death. Instead, as we saw with Agamben's discussion of ethics, we must begin from bare life as the remnant that cannot be eliminated or abandoned. It is in the experience of being bare life, in this radical experience of exposure, that we find our 'humanity'. To do this we must take up bare life, but not in the same way that power does. Where power separates out bare life and leaves it abandoned, any resistance to power must insist that we cannot be separated from bare life.

Once power isolates bare life, it then imposes on it social and legal identities. These are particular forms of life: 'social-juridical identities (the voter, the worker, the journalist, the student, but also the HIV-positive, the transvestite, the porno star, the elderly, the parent, the woman) that all rest on naked [bare] life' (ME: 6–7). Power operates by fragmenting and fracturing our identity, by constantly breaking the bond between our existence as living beings and our existence as speaking beings. In doing so this allows it to impose on us forms of life that locate us within particular identities. What remains constant, as the place in which this process of definition takes place, is the 'ground' of bare life. This means that our exposure to death is not something that simply takes place at the moment of our death. Instead, it is the place where our identity is constituted and these identities do not offer any real means for us to resist power. What we need to do is to find a new politics that lies outside the politics of bare life.

The alternative is what Agamben calls a 'form of life' where we find 'a life in which it is never possible to isolate something such as naked [bare] life' (ME: 3–4). If we take up bare life as a life that can never be separated from its form, then we have 'a form of life … [which] is wholly exhausted in bare life and a *bios* that is only its own *zoé* (HS: 188). The form of life refuses the isolation of bare life, which then allows the imposition of new political new identities. Instead it takes up the remnant of bare life as the place of a new politics of this remnant itself. Agamben will suggest that one place in which we can find this form of life is in the experience of the refugee. The refugee experiences the extreme disruption of their identity, and is left in a fragile and precarious state. As the postcolonial critic Robert Young points out, the refugee is the figure for the experience of modern culture: uprooted and left in the position where they can count on nothing (2003: 12). Although this is an extremely dangerous position, a position of almost complete exposure, Agamben also sees it as the place from which we can invent a new politics and new form of life that can challenge our exposure to death.

THE POLITICS OF THE REFUGEE

Why is the refugee so important today? Isn't the refugee one of the figures that is most exposed to power and to death? Agamben's reply to these questions is that the refugee is the crucial political category today for thinking a new politics in response to thanatopolitics. The claims he makes on behalf of the refugee are extensive:

> It is also the case that, given the by now unstoppable decline of the nation-state and the general corrosion of traditional political-juridical categories, the refugee is perhaps the only thinkable figure for the people of our time and the only category in which one may see today – at least until the process of dissolution of the nation-state and of its sovereignty has achieved full completion – the forms and limits of a coming political community. It is even possible that, if we want to be equal to the absolutely new tasks ahead, we will have to abandon decidedly, without reservation, the fundamental concepts through which we have so far represented the subjects of the political (man, the citizen and its rights, but also the sovereign people, the worker, and so forth) and build our political philosophy anew starting from the one and only figure of the refugee. (ME: 16)

He is arguing that, with the decline in secure political identities, it is the insecurity of the identity of the refugee that makes them the ideal figure of the people for our time. The fact that the refugee is robbed of a stable political identity is what makes them the foundation for a new political identity that can deal with the instability of modern culture.

Robert Young has stated that the refugee is 'an emblem of everything that people are experiencing in cold modernity across different times' (2003: 12), and Agamben would agree. If the *homo sacer* was the limit-concept of the Roman political order that allowed Agamben to reveal the original biopolitics of the Western culture of death, then the refugee is the limit-concept of modernity. The refugee is both the symptom of modernity, the extreme figure of bare life, and also what allows us to call the thanato-political culture of modernity into question. What sort of politics does the refugee promise us? Agamben argues that the politics of the refugee will be one that lies outside the state and also outside the legal order. This is because the refugee is not securely located within either the state law. The refugee is deprived of the protection of the state or law but, for this reason, he or she might allow us to discover or invent a new politics that would not depend on the state or law. The refugee offers the promise of a new coming political community that is not, simply, some new sort of national community but a community that is not built on an existing national, racial or legal identity.

The denial of the protection of the state and the denial of human rights to the refugee means that bare life need no longer be separated or excepted by power. All that is left for the refugee is bare life, and so they become this bare life. They cannot be separated from it because this is all they are. To find this new politics we must analyse the paradoxical 'position' of the refugee. On the one hand, the abandonment of the refugee, who is often left without legal or political rights, makes them supremely vulnerable. As we have seen, sovereign power works by exposing us and abandoning us to the risk of death. To be abandoned does not mean that we escape the clutches of power, but that we are held all the more closely by power. In fact, abandonment is how power penetrates into our being and strips away our political life to constitute us as bare life. Through being placed in this position we are then vulnerable to being ascribed an identity, one of the forms of life or 'social-juridical identities' that power can then impose upon us. On the other hand, it is this deprivation of political or social identity that makes the 'empty' identity of the refugee an almost pure example of bare life. In some sense, the refugee lives the fate of bare life, which we are all exposed to, more directly.

To be absolutely abandoned by power opens up the possibility of a new politics that escapes the limits of state and legal identity. Because the refugee is no longer securely inscribed within the state or law, they can become the figure of a bare or generic humanity. In Chapter Four, we explored how Agamben's new ethics of bare life turned to the figure of the camp inmate reduced to the abject status of the *Muselmann* ('Muslim'). Agamben claimed that this figure could testify to the fact that '*the one whose humanity is completely destroyed is the one who is truly human*' (RA: 133). In a similar way, it is the destruction of the political identity of the refugee that makes them truly the most political figure. They too have lost their 'humanity'; they have lost even the protection of 'universal' human rights, and are left with nothing. This 'nothing', this complete and total exposure to death and power, is *something*; it is the 'truly human'.

What the figure of the refugee offers is a new politics of exodus from power. This is not a politics of resistance, always bound to power and always bound to the body and life, but a politics of flight or fleeing from power. Although this is a politics of flight, it does not involve us fleeing from bare life. Instead, as with the 'Muslim', bare life is what is at stake as the site of the new politics and political struggle. With the refugee we can find a new 'form of life' that is also a new political life. Agamben explains that this is 'a life directed toward the idea of happiness and cohesive with a form of life' and that it is 'thinkable only starting with the emancipation from such a division [of bare life from politically qualified life], [and] with the irrevocable exodus from any sovereignty' (ME: 8). There are two conditions for the new politics of the refugee. First, it must refuse to divide or separate bare life from political life. It must refuse to act in the same way as sovereign power, which is constantly defining bare life and the division between bare life and political life. Secondly, it must be a politics that always flees from sovereignty and that refuses to remain within the politics of the state and of law.

The obvious problem is how are these transformations supposed to happen? Is it possible to go from the refugee as constituted by power to the refugee as the figure of a new politics? If the refugee is the figure that flees the exposure to death, then why is the refugee nearly always so exposed and so vulnerable to both power and the threat of death? These are critical questions, and Agamben is largely silent on how we might invent this new politics of the refugee. We could see this stance as similar to Foucault's refusal to fill out the category of resistance. In the same way, this new coming politics is a matter for practical invention and not theoretical description. Nor is the role of the lone political theorist to instruct us in a new communal politics, which will be a common effort. However, Agamben's silence means that it is possible to make a number of criticisms of this rather sketchy new politics. While Foucault's concept of resistance might not deal with our exposure to death, we could ask if this new politics of the refugee really leaves us in any better a position?

THE RISKS OF THE REFUGEE

What politics can the refugee offer us when, almost everywhere, the refugee is exposed to a bare power that operates with seeming impunity? Can the refugee elaborate any protest against power and how would it be articulated? The postcolonial critic Robert Young has been highly critical of the celebration of the exile, the migrant or the refugee by Western postmodernists (2003: 53). He says that the idea that these figures might offer new models of identity which are not based on physical links to family place may be all well and good for cosmopolitan intellectuals, but cannot be celebrated by those suffering in refugee camps. In contrast, Agamben is not celebrating the fate of the refugee, and he recognises the suffering and exposure they undergo as figures of bare life in modern culture. Instead, it is out of the desperate state of the refugee that Agamben sees hope emerging. Of course, we might still wonder whether this is a denial of the fate of the refugee and the difficulties that refugees face in constructing or inventing any politics at all. Certainly, if the politics of the refugee is communal, then this new political community will not only include refugees but emerge through the recognition that we are all exposed as bare life.

The second problem for this politics of the refugee is that it risks sentimentality. This is similar to the tendency to celebrate the plight of the refugee as a model of political identity. When we sentimentalise the refugee, we also minimise the problems they face in surviving, let alone practising politics. We also risk salving our own conscience by seeing them as some sort of vanguard political figure, instead of dealing with the practical problems they face in the here and now. One example of this risk of treating the refugee sentimentally is the Stephen Frears film *Dirty Pretty Things* (2003). In many ways this film is a very powerful and moving exploration of the plight of the refugee, focused on modern Britain. The film represents a diverse group of refugees trying to survive the threat of deportation and the various forms of exploitation that threaten them: exploitation of their labour, sexual exploitation, especially for women refugees, and even biological exploitation.

This last form of exploitation is explored through refugees being forced into the trade in organs to survive. Despite legal bans on organ trade, the demand for transplants in the West has often led to an illegal trade in organs from the third world. The refugee is not only reduced to selling their labour but also their body, either through prostitution or through the organ trade. The anthropologist Nancy Scheper Hughes has called this trade the 'new cannibalism' (1998). As she reports, and Frears's film dramatises, this trade is usually from the poor to the rich, and is especially prevalent in India and Brazil. Frears brings this trade into the first world, by having illegal operations carried out in a London hotel. He offers us a new understanding of the vulnerability and exploitation of bare life, this time at the economic level. What is more problematic is how the film constructs a vision of solidarity amongst its characters and offers us a relatively 'happy' ending. The characters unite around their common sense of exploitation and invisibility within the first world societies in which they have sought protection. Perhaps the difficulty with the ending of this film is also due to the 'resolution' demanded by the thriller genre, which is in conflict with the more political elements of the film. However, the vision of a community of refugees that it constructs seems sentimental, and the 'resistance' of the refugees lacks some credibility.

Agamben does not really risk sentimentality because he leaves his politics of the refugee in such an undefined state. What Frears's film demonstrates is the difficulty of constructing representations of the plight of the refugee that are accurate without simply either reducing them to victims or celebrating them as unlikely heroes. Is Agamben's refusal to confront the risks of the politics of the refugee a sign that he wants to keep clean hands in the face of intervening in such a complex and politically ambiguous global situation? I would suggest that we could see his politics of the refugee as empty but that this emptiness can be interpreted more positively. It may well be that the importance of the refugee is how this figure challenges our fundamental political concepts and exposes how all our political identities are founded on bare life. The refugee is the figure of the remnant of bare life that cannot be eliminated, but always remains. It is this 'position' of the refugee that demands that we invent a new politics. This politics must be realised as both practical and communal. If we are to deal with our fate as bare life, our fate as exposed to death, then we must create a new politics beginning from the remnant, from the refugee.

That this demand has yet to be really met is evident. However, in the mass protests against the Iraq war, it is possible to see something of a desire for an exodus from sovereign power, if not a new politics of the refugee. The slogan 'Not In Our Name' could indicate not only a temporary refusal of the way in which power is exercised but also a more global rejection of political identity itself. My suggestion, though, is at risk of trying to fill out the space of this new politics. What is true is that any such politics has, after Agamben, to face the problem of modern death. In doing so we must recognise that death is not the limit to power or something taboo, as Foucault thought. Instead, death is still at the heart of power and the 'old powers of death' have not so much waned but have transformed and been extended. It is the spreading of this power across the political space of modern culture that makes it so hard to track and face. These new forms of exposure to death must be carefully analysed, but this analysis should also connect to a practical and communal politics of bare life. The culture of death is not simply a matter for theorists or academics but something that leaves all of us exposed in new ways.

CONCLUSION: APPROACHING MODERN DEATH

In the conclusion to this chapter the threads of my analysis of the culture of death will be gathered together. I began, in Chapter One, by approaching modern death through our exposure to the instability in our experience of the time of death. This experience of instability was introduced by the threat of mass politically and bureaucratically organised death in modern culture. The two primary events that shape this sense of exposure are the concentration camps and the threat of nuclear war: 'Auschwitz' and 'Hiroshima'. Although the dividing line between life and death has always been vague and unstable, this instability takes a new form in modern culture. The work of Giorgio Agamben helped define this instability by locating it in bare life. What this demonstrates is that political identity is founded on an exposure to death and that this political definition of life and death has spread to all political identity in modern culture. Therefore the alteration in the time of death concerns both a shift in our exposure to death and the individual experience of this exposure. The impact of this suggestion is that we must pursue the forms that this exposure to death might take, and whether these forms of exposure are enough to define a modern culture of death.

I then analysed these new forms of exposure through the spaces of power in which they are exercised. In Chapter Two, this involved us returning to the analysis of the nature of power, and how power might be linked to the problem of death. Against Foucault's argument that power finds its limit in death, I used Agamben's analysis to demonstrate how power still remains a matter of life and death. This is most evident if we consider the concentration camps. Agamben's controversial argument that the camps are not confined to the past but are permanent possibilities of power in modern culture forces us to rethink our exposure to death. Although his argument is problematic, the reappearance of new forms of the camp, whether in the war in the former Yugoslavia or during the 'war against terrorism', suggests that we must try to analyse the legal and political space of the camp. This should not involve minimising or 'relativising' the Nazi death camps, but it should involve close attention to how the exposure to power and to death takes place. No approach to our culture of death can ignore these issues.

In Chapter Three, this analysis was further refined through a close examination of one of the places in which we are exposed to death today: the hospital room. Focusing in particular on the issue of patients sustained by life-support allows us to bring together the problem of the time of death with the problem of the space of death. These two problems converge on the further politicisation of death in modern culture. Although death has always been political, we can see how, in modern culture, this politics of death (thanatopolitics) exposes us all to death. This new, more extreme exposure to death might well be a way in which we can characterise modern death. Certainly this claim would require further development and more detailed historical evidence. There is no doubt that Agamben overstates some of his claims, or does not provide adequate evidence for them. However, the politicising of death allows us to grasp how the new forms of exposure to death in modern culture might well be linked together and why they might constitute a new modern death.

The second half of the book explored the possible responses to our exposure to death at this mass level. In Chapter Four, I remained in the hospital room to examine the attempt by bioethicists to construct an ethics of modern death that would allow us to come to terms with the new forms of exposure to death. The problem with these attempts is that they do not pose the problem of death as political but instead rely on an ethical discourse to solve problems of power. New critical readings of the ethical turn in contemporary culture suggest the dangers of such approaches, which still leave us exposed to death. Agamben's own ethics of bare life at least has the merit of taking this exposure to death as the critical issue, and of not minimising its political dimension. Certainly his new ethics does not seem to offer us enough in the way of practical advice in how to deal with death. Its advantage is that it insists that any ethics of death must begin from the experience of bare life. Bare life is where we find our humanity today, and any ethics that excludes bare life can be seen as repeating the gesture of sovereign power.

Chapter Five examined the celebration of death as a transgressive experience in contemporary art. This celebration can be understood as the result of our exposure to death as bare life in modern culture. What is problematic is that it remains bewitched by bare life and fascinated with the threat of mass death. Although it might make that threat visible, quite literally, it leaves the politics of modern death invisible. The desire to shock and scandalise, the desire to find in the confrontation with death an experience of intensity, is actually quite limited. What we need to do is to move beyond an aesthetics of transgressive death (Bataille), or an aesthetics of intense life (Bacon/ Deleuze), to an aesthetics of bare life. I suggested that the profane and banal death in the car crash might be a better model of death in modern culture than the extreme experiences on which artists have so often concentrated. This is not to deny or ignore the need for an aesthetics of modern death, as Agamben seems to do. Instead, it is to suggest that the aesthetics of bare life is an aesthetics of exposure: the exposure to a banal and profane death.

In this final chapter, I have turned to the politics of resistance to modern death. If the boundary between life and death is political, then it may well be that we need a politics of modern death to resist the new forms of our exposure to death. However, the value of resistance is problematic, especially when that resistance to power is located in the body or in life. The problem is that this resistance does not deal with bare life, but celebrates bare life as the site of resistance. As we rethought power in the light of death in Chapter Two, so now we have had to rethink resistance in the light of death in this chapter. It may well be that the value of resistance is exhausted in the face of our exposure to death and that we need a new politics of exodus from power. This politics is extremely ambiguous and has hardly even been developed yet. To develop it further, and so to gauge its worth, is not just a matter of critical analysis but also of practical and communal politics. The theorist cannot stand in for the practice of politics, but must encourage new and inventive modes of communal thinking that might allow us to think beyond the modern culture of death.

I am not sure that it is possible to end on the reversal of the desperate state of the current situation into a new hope, as Agamben suggests. We might well actually require more careful and extended analysis of the culture of death, which contests some of the limits of our contemporary thinking. One way to do this, which I have used here, is to approach modern death through the concept of our exposure to death. This approach has no pretence to solving the problem of modern death or offering the definitive account of the contemporary culture of death. Instead, it is a critical starting point that I have developed to try and come to terms with the widespread sense of our exposure to death after Auschwitz and Hiroshima, and in the current time of the 'war against terrorism'. The model of exposure to death allows us to recast the culture of death, to approach our history and the present in new ways. Perhaps it might also allow us to challenge both the visibility and invisibility of death in modern culture, and to analyse the culture of death as the culture of our survival in the face of the exposure to death.

NOTES

1. Claire Colebrook's *Gilles Deleuze* (2002) is a concise introduction to his philosophy as a philosophy of life.

Conclusion: The Meaning of Death

If modern death can be approached through the question of our exposure to death, then does this have implications for the study of death more generally? In this conclusion I shall argue that this approach may undermine the obsessive search for the meaning of death in Western culture. This search for the meaning of death can still be found in discourses that claim to analyse the nature of death, such as death studies. In death studies the search has been for the historically and culturally determined meanings of death, and the nature of death itself has been left aside. For example, in their introduction to the collection *Death and Representation* (1993), the critics Goodwin and Bronfen argue that: 'Death is thus necessarily constructed by a culture; it grounds the many ways a culture stabilizes and represents itself, and yet it always does so as a signifier with an incessantly receding, ungraspable signified, always pointing to other signifiers, other means of representing what finally is absent' (1993: 4). What is combined in this approach is the idea that death is culturally constructed through particular meanings. Death is a matter of language, of signifiers that circle around death as absence. In this way death itself is lost to us, and it is left as ungraspable.

The problems with the death studies approach can be seen as due to this combination of seeing death as a matter of shifting cultural meanings that circle around death itself as an ungraspable and mysterious core. In focusing on the cultural meaning of death, what is lost is any reflection on how the boundary between death and life is fixed politically. Instead of interrogating how this shifting boundary is put into place, death studies too often remains studying the boundary in terms of its cultural meaning. In fact, as I have suggested, our exposure to death must be considered through an analysis of how the boundary between life and death becomes put into place. This exposure is not primarily about shifting cultural meanings but about how the politics of life and death leaves us exposed to death. To do this I have often turned to the work of the Italian philosopher Giorgio Agamben. Although his work is problematic, it does offer us some provocative new ways in which to approach death.

Too often, when we approach death, we are left with the infinite task of searching out the changing meanings of death, and death itself recedes further and further from our grasp. Strangely, although the stated aim is to explore the culture of death, the result is that death itself is left at the limit of culture, or outside it. Death becomes consigned to the position of the zero point of our culture, and then the culture of death is something which is constructed on this fundamental absence. We are left with no real access to death at all, and rather than providing us with an analysis of the culture of death all we are left with is an analysis of cultural meanings of death. The question could be asked, is death studies actually really about death? Doesn't it presuppose that we know what death is? In fact, it seems confident in regarding death as a physical event that can never really be grasped in itself. Although this leaves it as mysterious, it does presume that we can know that death cannot be known. We could even say that death in death studies occupies a similar position to bare life in Western culture: inclusive exclusion.

This is because death is included in death studies as its 'object' of analysis. Death studies includes death by presuming the possibility of us grasping the vast and shifting meanings of death in our and other cultures. It presumes the possibility of charting cultural shifts in 'death' across time, and within and between cultures. However, the slippage is that it is not so much discussing death as the meaning of death. This means that death itself is left excluded by death studies. It is excluded because it is consigned to the position of the ungraspable physical event that lies beyond any cultural meaning. The fact that death seems to occupy this position of inclusive exclusion in relation to death studies could well be seen as the result of power. What death studies tends to do is repeat the operation of sovereign power, which operates through the inclusive exclusion of bare life. This would be another confirmation of the spread of sovereign power throughout modern culture, even into the ways in which we think. The implication of death studies repeating the operation of power is that this means that it cannot grasp bare life. When it repeats the function of power, it loses the possibility of thinking about our exposure to death, an exposure that penetrates our very existence.

The work of Giorgio Agamben warns us of this danger and opens the possibility of probing death itself as exposure, rather than leaving it in the strange position of inclusive exclusion. By leaving it in the strange position of that which can be grasped, but which also always escapes our grasp, death studies also risks leaving us in a state of fascination with death. Instead of moving to grasp death and grasp our exposure to death, we are left with the endless pursuit of the changing meanings of death, and the fascination with an underlying and ungraspable death that can never be found. Certainly, as I have tried to chart in this work, this fascination with death, in terms of the meaning of death, appears everywhere. Today, this fascination extends from artists and philosophers to the speculations on death of so-called ordinary people (see Terkel, 2002). This is true not only of modern culture of course, but in modern culture I have tried to analyse how this fascination might have altered under the impact of new forms of our exposure to death. As we become exposed to death in new ways, and to the extent this exposure penetrates all political identity, then the fascination of death becomes even more pressing. Death is at once feared and desired, an object of disgust and horror, but also of pleasure. In these ways what is avoided, though, is the profane banality of death.

This means that our fascination with death does not necessarily indicate that we have really begun to analyse death, and it might well be the sign of our resistance to analysing death. Our fascination with death means we are left transfixed before it, clutching at its different meanings but leaving death itself unexamined. One way in which Agamben's work is useful is that it can help us break with this fascination. By beginning from the problem of life towards the experience of life exposed to death, Agamben helps us to take a 'detour' that might actually lead to a more direct approach to death. In doing so, he helps us avoid the endless dispute on the meaning or non-meaning of death in which we so often appear to be trapped. Whether we are trying to find the meaning of death or decrying or celebrating death as meaningless we are still avoiding death. Death is constantly left deferred.

This is not to underestimate the difficulty of approaching death or to dismiss out of hand the work carried out in death studies. As I have stressed throughout this book, approaches like that of Agamben do not offer any straightforward solution to the problems of the culture of death. In fact, his approach generates a new series of problems, but these problems might well be productive ways in which to consider death in a new light. I have mentioned various specific problems with Agamben's account of bare life and our exposure to death. One of the general problems of his work, which is especially relevant at this point, is his tendency to give death a political meaning. How can I argue that Agamben helps us to avoid our obsession with the meaning of death if he just provides death with another meaning? Despite this problem, his work on our exposure to death in modern culture helps us to begin an analysis of the culture of death as the culture of our exposure to death.

It is his political reading of death that allows him to approach death as exposure by specifying, in some ways, how power leaves us exposed to death and how death is always a matter of power. His pursuit of these problems from the position of life allows us a new understanding of the culture of death, and how this culture touches on a range of questions and discourses that might, initially, seem remote from it: ethics, art, philosophy, politics, etc. However, he does make the exposure to death political in the last instance. It is politics that plays the crucial role in deciding on the time of death, of exercising itself in places where we are exposed to death, and of politicising death through and through. In modern culture this exposure appears to have spread and to have taken new forms that penetrate into our political identities. This is what Agamben calls the 'zone of indistinction', in which we are all virtually bare life, we are all exposed to death, and we are all, also, exposed to the power that decides on life and death, from birth to the moment of our actual death.

This exposure to death is not evenly distributed, as Agamben might sometimes appear to be suggesting. Some of us are more exposed to death than others, and even the new forms of our exposure to death often tend to follow the usual vectors of power: class, 'race', gender and sexuality. However, he also suggests that what is radical about our exposure to death by power in modern culture is that it has become central to all of us, no matter how privileged we might be. This is clear from the example of the Spanish head of state General Franco. For all his political power, he was left at the mercy of the politics of bare life embodied today in the power of doctors. This leaves us with a new problem, summarised by the philosopher Slavoj Zizek: 'the true problem is not the fragile status of the excluded but, rather, the fact that, on the most elementary level, we are *all* "excluded" in the sense that our most elementary "zero" position is that of an object of biopolitics' (2002: 95).

This is why it is necessary to recognise the importance of politics to the decision on the time of death, and so to the culture of death. If we are all faced with the fate of being bare life, then we cannot escape the problem of the operation of sovereign power. In this sense the politics of the refugee, which we explored in Chapter Six, is not only a politics for refugees. Although refugees are exposed to the power of death to an extreme degree, they simply figure the potential fate of any of us. This means that the politics of the refugee is the politics of all of us, it concerns all of us and it must be the starting point for any new politics. It also means that the issue of our exposure to death is not only an issue for academic debate and analysis. The exposure to death is a pressing issue that we must all face, unless we are to remain as the 'excluded' and exposed to death in these radical ways. However, perhaps we need to go further than leaving our exposure to death as political. We need to go further in analysing the history of the culture of death in terms of the exposure to death to grasp how different our modern culture of death really is. In addition, we need to grasp more precisely the mechanisms by which we are exposed to death and the places in which these mechanisms operate.

These are questions that Agamben has opened but not sufficiently developed. His work must be integrated within the wider field of death studies to produce a more nuanced reading of the history of death as exposure. This includes widening his work to consider how we are exposed to death in particular spaces of power, and how this exposure to death is represented in both high and popular culture, as I have done in this study. Agamben might allow us to interrogate the limits of the culture of death in new ways but we must also question the limits of his own account as well. In particular, we must consider whether the political meaning of death is what really exhausts the problem of death and whether it allows us to focus on death itself. This does not mean that we must ignore the political elements of death, which his work makes so clear. These elements have been confirmed by the operations of contemporary power. In the 'new military humanism' (Chomsky) of global power and in its 'right' to intervene wherever and whenever it detects a threat to its operation, we can see the evidence of thanatopolitical power. This extension of global power prompts us to push this exploration of death as exposure further.

In Chapter Five, I examined how the problem of the exposure to death has been taken up in modern art and how this exposure could leave any account of the meaning of death as problematic, including Agamben's. We saw how the exposure to death could leave death exposed to us, beyond the issues of the meaning of death or of death as meaningless. In this stripping away of the meaning of death by modern art, we are left exposed to death outside any evasions that meaning, or non-meaning, could leave us with. This experience is very close to what the philosopher Simon Critchley has called 'meaninglessness as an achievement' in his book Very Little ... Almost Nothing (1997: 27). This book, which analyses the responses of philosophers and artists to death, argues that we need to move away from any heroic approach to death. It also argues that, instead, we should approach our exposure to death in a more everyday way. However, despite the value of this deflation of our fascination with death, his call for seeing meaninglessness as achievement is problematic.

Although Critchley avoids the pathos of heroism, celebration and fascina-tion often associated with death by seeking this achievement in the ordinary, he does not escape from still approaching death through meaning. The assumption from which he begins is that we must find meaning in death if 'death is not just going to have the character of a brute fact' (Critchley, 1997: 25). He then goes on to argue that this desire for meaning is a problem, and it should be replaced by the achievement of meaninglessness instead. This achievement of meaninglessness can best be found in the works of the Irish writer Samuel Beckett (1906–1989). His novels, plays and radio works all probe how the meaninglessness of life and death dominate our experience, to the point where Beckett himself said that every word he wrote was an 'unnecessary stain on silence and nothingness'. At the same time, through writing, he recorded this experience of meaninglessness, and that was his achievement. However, the 'achievement of meaninglessness' is not really an escape from the quest for the meaning of death but another twist on it. As we saw with death studies, the search for the meaning of death can work alongside the idea that death is fundamentally meaningless with little difficulty.

Critchley stresses the profane banality of death, seeing it as 'very little … almost nothing' but this 'almost nothing' may still be too much! What he avoids is the idea that death may well be only a brute fact. The exposure to death in modern culture has made clearer the idea that death is a brute fact, and that this brute fact cannot be understood in terms of either the meaning of death or the meaninglessness of death. It is the banality and profane nature of modern death, or that modern death makes evident the banal and profane nature of death, which allows us to analyse death as exposure. In particular, what I called, in Chapter Five, the aesthetics of bare life, approaches our exposure to death as pure exposure. This exposure exhausts the meaning of death, because it exhausts sense and meaning. The attempt to recover the meaning of death or to recover death as the 'achievement of meaninglessness' evades this exposure and the exhaustion death faces us with. If we are to analyse death as exposure, then we might well have to analyse death outside the idea of meaning or non-meaning.

To do this we would have to precisely specify the mechanisms and forms by which we are exposed to death and what this exposure actually is. In this book I have tried to begin doing this, and suggested that in modern culture this situation exposes us to death in new ways, particularly in the forms of politically and bureaucratically organised mass death. Now modern death becomes the foundation of all political identity; it pursues us into the hospital room and into our very sense of existence. This exposure to death also cuts through some of the previous ways in which death has been approached. Of course, it certainly cannot claim to completely resolve or evade the problems of these previous approaches. To talk of our exposure to death could be seen as another attempt to impose meaning on death. I hope, though, it opens up different questions and the possibility of approaching death as 'brute fact', as well as helping us to recognise the political dimension of our exposure to death.

It forces us to revise our concepts and to interrogate a whole range of academic disciplines. Death as exposure exposes contemporary thought to problems that it has yet to properly engage with. From history to sociology, cultural studies to philosophy, in both high and popular culture, we can find traces of this exposure. To reconsider the profane banality of death, something that modern death poses acutely, is to try and produce a new kind of analysis and writing of death. This new writing of death must constantly challenge the fascination of death and the heroism that is often associated with 'confronting' death. In fact, the whole language of confrontation, to which this study has not been immune, may need to be discarded. The brutality of the brute fact of death calls us to try and produce a new writing of death that can recognise this brutality, but also challenge the brutality of power that constantly decides on life and death. These problems are posed in the most concrete way in modern culture; they are also posed with great urgency. The analysis of death becomes more and more pressing as the new global reach of power leaves us all exposed to death.

Bibliography

Adams, P. (2003), 'Art as Prosthesis: Cronenberg's *Crash*' in P. Adams (ed.), *Art: Sublimation or Symptom*, London and New York: Karnac.

Agamben, G. (1998), *Homo Sacer: Sovereign Power and Bare Life*, trans. D. Heller-Roazen, Stanford, California: Stanford University Press. [HS]

—— (1999a), *Potentialities: Collected Essays in Philosophy*, trans. and intro. D. Heller-Roazen, Stanford, California: Stanford University Press. [P]

—— (1999b), *Remnants of Auschwitz: the Witness and the Archive*, trans. D. Heller-Roazen, New York: Zone Books. [RA]

—— (2000), *Means without End: Notes on Politics*, trans. V. Binetti and C. Casarino, Minneapolis and London: University of Minnesota Press. [ME]

Ariès, P. (1974), *Western Attitudes toward Death from the Middle Ages to the Present*, trans. P. M. Ranum, London and New York: Marion Boyars.

—— (1981), *The Hour of Our Death*, trans. H. Weaver, New York: Alfred A. Knopf.

Badiou, A. (2001), *Ethics: An Essay on the Understanding of Evil*, trans. and intro. P. Hallward, London and New York: Verso.

Ballard, J. G. (1975), *Crash*, London: Panther Books.

Bataille, G. (1985), 'The Practice of Joy Before Death' [1939] in A. Stoekl (ed.), *Visions of Excess: Selected Writings, 1927–1939*, trans. A. Stoekl, C. R. Lovitt and D. M. Leslie Jr, Minneapolis: University of Minnesota Press.

—— (1989), *The Tears of Eros*, trans. P. Connor, San Francisco: City Lights Books.

—— (1990), 'Hegel, Death and Sacrifice', trans. J. Strauss, in A. Stoekl (ed.), *On Bataille*, *Yale French Studies*, 78: 9–28.

Baudrillard, J. (1993), *Symbolic Exchange and Death*, trans. I. H. Grant, intro. M. Gane, London, Thousand Oaks, New Delhi: Sage.

—— (1994), *Simulacra and Simulation*, trans. S. F. Glaser, Ann Arbor: The University of Michigan Press.

Bauman, Z. (1991), *Modernity and the Holocaust*, Cambridge: Polity.

Berridge, K. (2002), *Vigor Mortis: The End of the Death Taboo*, London: Profile Books.

Beyst, S. (2002), 'Hermann Nitsch's *"Orgien Mysterien Theater"*: The Artist as High Priest?', http://d-sites.net/english/nitsch.htm.

Bosworth, R. J. B. (1994), *Explaining Auschwitz and Hiroshima*, London and New York: Routledge.

Bronfen, E. (1992), *Over Her Dead Body: Death, Femininity and the Aesthetic*, Manchester: Manchester University Press.

Brottman, M. (ed.) (2001), *Car-Crash Culture*, New York: Palgrave.

Buñuel, L. (1985), *My Last Breath*, trans. A. Israel, London: Fontana.

Burleigh, M. (1994), *Death and Deliverance: 'Euthanasia' in Germany 1900–1945*, Cambridge: Cambridge University Press.

Butler, R. (1999), *Jean Baudrillard: The Defence of the Real*, London, Thousand Oaks, New Delhi: Sage.

Camus, A. (1975), *The Myth of Sisyphus*, trans. J. O'Brien, Harmondsworth: Penguin.

Chomsky, N. (1999), *The New Military Humanism*, London and Sterling, Virginia: Pluto.

Colebrook, C. (2002), *Gilles Deleuze*, London and New York: Routledge.

Critchley, S. (1997), *Very Little … Almost Nothing*, London and New York: Routledge.

Deleuze, G. (1988), *Foucault*, trans. and ed. Seán Hand, London: The Athlone Press.

—— (1997), 'Immanence: A Life…', trans. N. Millett, *Theory, Culture and Society*, 14, 2: 3–7.

—— (2003), *Francis Bacon: the Logic of Sensation*, trans. D. W. Smith, London and New York: Continuum.

—— and Guattari, F. (1988), *A Thousand Plateaus*, trans. Brian Massumi, London: Athlone Press.

DeLillo, D. (1985), *White Noise*, London: Picador.

Derrida, J. (1993), *Aporias*, trans. T. Dutoit, Stanford, California: Stanford University Press.

—— (2001), *The Work of Mourning*, trans. P.-A. Brault and M. Naas, Chicago: The University of Chicago Press.

Dickens, C. (1997), *Our Mutual Friend* [1865], ed. and intro. A. Poole, London: Penguin.

Dollimore, J. (1998), *Death, Desire and Loss in Western Culture*, London: Penguin.

Eliot, T. S. (1963), *Collected Poems 1909–1962*, London: Faber & Faber.

Fitzpatrick, P. (2001), '"These mad abandon'd times"', *Economy and Society*, 30, 2: 255–70.

Foucault, M. (1979a), *The History of Sexuality: An Introduction*, trans. R. Hurley, Harmondsworth: Penguin.

—— (1979b), *Discipline and Punish*, trans. A. Sheridan, Harmondsworth: Penguin.

—— (1989a), *The Birth of the Clinic*, trans. A. M. Sheridan, London and New York: Tavistock/Routledge.

—— (1989b), *Foucault Live*, New York: Semiotext(e).

—— (2003), *'Society Must Be Defended': Lectures at the Collège de France, 1975–76*, trans. D. Macey, ed. M. Bertani and A. Fontana, London: Penguin.

Gide, A. (1969), *The Vatican Cellars*, trans. D. Bussy, Harmondsworth: Penguin.

Goodwin, S. W. and E. Bronfen (1993), 'Introduction' in S. W. Goodwin and E. Bronfen (eds), *Death and Representation*, Baltimore and London: Johns Hopkins University Press.

Hallward, P. (2003), *Badiou: a Subject to Truth*, Minneapolis and London: University of Minnesota Press.

Haraway, D. (1999), 'The Cyborg Manifesto' in S. During (ed.), *The Cultural Studies Reader*, 2nd edn, London and New York: Routledge.

Harris, T. (1999), *Hannibal*, London: William Heinemann.

Hegarty, P. (2000), *Bataille: Core Cultural Theorist*, London, Thousand Oaks, New Delhi: Sage.

Hilberg, R. (1985), *The Destruction of the European Jews*, student edn, New York and London: Holmes & Meier.

Houlbrooke, R. (1998), *Death, Religion and the Family in England 1480–1750*, Oxford: Clarendon.

Hughes, N. S. (1998), 'The New Cannibalism', *New Internationalist* 300, http://www.newint.org/issue300/trade.html.

Ince, K. (2000), *Orlan: Millennial Female*, Oxford and New York: Berg.

Jalland, P. (1999), 'Victorian Death and its Decline: 1850–1918' in P. C. Jupp and C. Gittings (eds), *Death in England: An Illustrated History*, Manchester: Manchester University Press.

James, P. D. (1977), *The Black Tower*, London: Sphere.

Kafka, F. (2000), *The Trial* [1925], trans. I. Parry, London: Penguin.

Keats, J. (1996), *Selected Poems*, ed. N. Roe, London: J. M. Dent.

Kuhse, H. and Singer, P. (eds) (1998), *A Companion to Bioethics*, Oxford and Malden, Mass.: Blackwell.

Lesy, M. (2000), *Wisconsin Death Trip* [1973], Alburquerque, New Mexico: University of New Mexico Press.

Levi, P. (1988), *The Drowned and the Saved*, London: Abacus.

Mailer, N. (1968), 'The White Negro' [1957], in *Advertisements for Myself*, London: Panther.

Martin, E. A. (ed.) (2003), *Oxford Concise Medical Dictionary*, 6th edn, Oxford: Oxford University Press.

Miah, A. (2003), 'Dead Bodies for the Masses: The British Public Autopsy and the Aftermath', *Ctheory* 26, 1–2, http://www.ctheory.net.

Miller, J. (1993), *The Passion of Michel Foucault*, New York: Simon and Schuster.

Mitford, J. (1998), *The American Way of Death Revisited*, London: Virago.

Noys, B. (1998), 'Transgressing Transgression: The Limits of Bataille's Fiction' in Larry Duffy and Adrian Tudor (eds), *Les Lieux Interdits: Transgression and French Literature*, Hull: Hull University Press.

—— (2003), 'Badiou's Fidelities: Reading the *Ethics*', *Communication and Cognition*, 36, 1 & 2: 31–44.

Palahniuk, C. (2003), *Diary: A Novel*, London: Jonathan Cape.

Poe, E. A. (1993), *Tales of Mystery and Imagination*, London and Vermont: Everyman.

—— (1999), 'The Philosophy of Composition', www.eapoe.org/essays/philcomp.htm.

Preston, P. (1995), *Franco*, London: Fontana.

Reynolds, A. (2002), *Diamond Dogs, Turquoise Days*, London: Gollancz.

Richardson, S. (1928), *Familiar Letters on Important Occasions*, London: George Routledge and Sons.

Roseman, M. (2002), *The Villa, the Lake, the Meeting: Wansee and the Final Solution*, London: Penguin Books.

Said, E. (1995), *Orientalism*, Harmondsworth: Penguin.

—— (2002), 'In Conversation' in D. T. Goldberg and A. Quayson (eds), *Relocating Postcolonialism*, Oxford: Blackwell.

Schaefer, S. (2003), 'What the NYTs Choose Not to Mention: Italian Philosopher Giorgio Agamben Protests US Travel Policies', *Counterpunch*, http://www.counterpunch.org/schaeffer01232004.html.

Sereny, G. (2000), *The German Trauma*, London: Allen Lane.

Sierz, A. (2001), *In-Yer-Face Theatre*, London: Faber & Faber.

Singer, P. (1994), *Rethinking Life and Death*, Oxford: Oxford University Press.

—— (2002), *Unsanctifying Life*, ed. and intro. H. Kuhse, Oxford and Malden, Mass.: Blackwell.

Terkel, S. (2002), *Will the Circle Be Unbroken?*, London: Granta Books.

Virilio, P. (2002), *Ground Zero*, trans. C. Turner, London and New York: Verso.

—— (2003), *Art and Fear*, trans. Julie Rose, intro. John Armitage, London and New York: Continuum.

Young, Robert J. C. (2003), *Postcolonialism: A Very Short Introduction*, Oxford: Oxford University Press.

Zizek, S. (2002), *Welcome to the Desert of the Real!*, London and New York: Verso.

—— (2003), *The Puppet and the Dwarf*, Cambridge, Mass. and London: The MIT Press.

—— and Dolar, M. (2002), *Opera's Second Death*, London and New York: Routledge.

FILMOGRAPHY

Apocalypse Now (1979), Directed by Francis Ford Coppola, USA: American Zoetrope.

Coma (1977), Directed by Michael Crichton, USA: Warner Studios.

Crash (1996), Directed by David Cronenberg, USA: Columbia Tristar.

Dawn of the Dead (1979), Directed by George A. Romero, USA.

Dawn of the Dead (2004), Directed by Zack Snyder, USA: Universal Studios.

Day of the Dead (1985), Directed by George A. Romero, USA.

Dead Ringers (1988), Directed by David Cronenberg, USA.

Dirty Pretty Things (2003), Directed by Stephen Frears, UK: Miramax.

Night of the Living Dead (1969), Directed by George A. Romero, USA.

Return of the Living Dead (1984), Directed by Dan O'Bannon, USA.

The Act of Seeing with One's Own Eyes (1971), Directed by Stan Brakhage, USA.

The Ring (1998), Directed by Hideo Nakata, Japan.

28 Days Later (2002), Directed by Danny Boyle, UK: Fox Searchlight Pictures.

Wisconsin Death Trip (1999), Directed by James Marsh, UK: BBC Arena and Cinemax.

INTERNET SITES

www.amnesty.org (viewed March 2004), reports on Camp Delta in Guantánamo Bay, Cuba.

http://www.bodyworlds.com/en/pages/home.asp (viewed March 2004), the web site for Gunther Von Hagens's Body World exhibition.

http://www.cbs.com/primetime/csi/main.shtml (viewed March 2004), the official web site of the CBS television series *Crime Scene Investigation.*

http://www.inyerface-theatre.com/intro.html (viewed March 2004), web site of Aleks Sierz dealing with 'in-yer-face' theatre, including the work of Sarah Kane.

http://www.orlan.net/ (viewed March 2004), web site of the 'transgenic' artist Orlan (in French).

http://www.stelarc.va.com.au (viewed March 2004), web site of the Australian transgenic artist Stelarc.

www.ushmm.org/ (viewed March 2004), web site of the United States Holocaust Memorial Museum, America's national institution for the documentation, study and interpretation of Holocaust history.

http://www.who2.com/deathbycarcrash.html (viewed March 2004), celebrity car-crash deaths.

www.wisconsindeathtrip.com/ (viewed March 2004), the web site of James Marsh's 1999 film *Wisconsin Death Trip*.

http://www.yad-vashem.org.il/ (viewed March 2004), the web site of Yad Vashem, the Holocaust Martyrs' and Heroes' Remembrance Authority.

Index